the
educator's
book
of
quotes

CORWIN PRESS

The Corwin Press logo—a raven striding across an open book—represents the happy union of courage and learning. We are a professional-level publisher of books and journals for K-12 educators, and we are committed to creating and providing resources that embody these qualities. Corwin's motto is "Success for All Learners."

the
educator's
book
of
quotes

JOHN BLAYDES

CORWIN PRESS, INC.
A Sage Publications Company
Thousand Oaks, California

For information:

 Corwin Press, Inc.
A Sage Publications Company
2455 Teller Road
Thousand Oaks, California 91320
www.corwinpress.com

Sage Publications Ltd.
6 Bonhill Street
London EC2A 4PU
United Kingdom

Sage Publications India Pvt. Ltd.
B-42, Panchsheel Enclave
Post Box 4109
New Delhi 110 017 India

Printed in the United States of America

Library of Congress Cataloging-in-Publication Data

The Educator's book of quotes/[compiled] by John Blaydes
    p. cm.
ISBN 0-7619-3862-1 (cloth)
ISBN 0-7619-3863-X (pbk.)
  1. Education—Quotations, maxims, etc. 2. Conduct of life—Quotations, maxims, etc. I. Blaydes, John. II. Title.
PN6084.E38E38 2003
370—dc21

                         2002156469

This book is printed on acid-free paper.

03 04 05 06 10 9 8 7 6 5 4 3 2 1

Acquisitions Editor:	Robert D. Clouse
Associate Editor:	Kristen L. Gibson
Editorial Assistants:	Erin Clow, Jingle Vea
Copy Editor:	Teresa Herlinger
Production Editor:	Denise Santoyo
Typesetter:	C&M Digitals (P) Ltd.
Cover Designer:	Michael Dubowe

CONTENTS

PREFACE

For me, quotes are nuggets of wit and wisdom that motivate and inspire. The discovery of new, meaningful quotes is always a delightful surprise. As a "quote collector," my favorite quotes were scattered in various files and underlined in dozens of books, which often made it difficult to find the right quote when I needed it.

The purpose of this book is to provide one central resource to which educators can quickly turn for a compilation of quotes relating to education and leadership. The quotes are organized for easy access and referenced by themes.

—*John Blaydes*

ABOUT
THE AUTHOR

 **John Blaydes** is one of the nation's foremost experts in the field of school administration. He is an inspirational leader, author, motivational speaker, seminar leader, and educational consultant.

In recognition of his innovative leadership, Blaydes has been honored with both the National Distinguished School Principal Award and the prestigious Milken Foundation National Educator Award. He also received the Kennedy Center for the Performing Arts National School Administrator Award for his dedication to arts education and the School Principal Leadership Award from the California Librarians Association for his outstanding media center program.

In his role as inspirational leader, he has promoted a culture of excellence. His school was twice selected as a California Distinguished School and has been honored with multiple awards for its outstanding visual and performing arts, media center, and math programs. Staff awards garnered by his school include the National School Nurse of the Year, the Presidential Award for Excellence in Mathematics Teaching, the California Media Center Teacher of the Year, the Sallie Mae First Year Teacher Award, the Orange County Teacher of the Year, and another Milken Foundation National Educator Award.

Blaydes has a broad array of experience in educational leadership, having been a classroom teacher, school site principal, district office administrator, and elected school board member in his community.

Other Books by John Blaydes

Inspirational Leadership—Creating a Culture of Excellence in Times of Change (1998)

Enhancing Your Effectiveness as an Elementary School Principal (1996)

INSPIRATION

I quote others only the
better to express myself.

—Michel de Montaigne,
Essayist

When one door of happiness closes, another opens; but often we look so long at the closed door that we do not see the one which has been opened for us.

—Helen Keller

⚬⚬⚬⚬⚬⚬⚬⚬

There are high spots in all of our lives and most of them come about through encouragement from someone else. Encouragement is oxygen to the soul.

—George Matthew Adams,
Author

⚬⚬⚬⚬⚬⚬⚬⚬

Let each of us aspire to inspire, before we expire.

—Albert Clarke Jr.,
Author

⚬⚬⚬⚬⚬⚬⚬⚬

Whether you think you can or think you can't, you're right.

—Henry Ford

⚬⚬⚬⚬⚬⚬⚬⚬

In everyone's life, at some time our inner fire goes out. It is then burst into flame by an encounter with another human being. We should all be thankful for those people who rekindle the inner spirit.

—Albert Schweitzer,
Humanitarian, Missionary

The grand essentials of happiness are: something to do, something to love, and something to hope for.

—Allan. K. Chalmers,
Author

~~~~~~~~~~~

Genius is one percent inspiration and ninety-nine percent perspiration.

—Thomas Edison

~~~~~~~~~~~

You gain strength, courage, and confidence by every experience in which you really stop to look fear in the face.

—Eleanor Roosevelt

~~~~~~~~~~~

Life isn't about the breaths we take, it's about the moments that take our breath away.

—Author Unknown

~~~~~~~~~~~

When everything seems to be going against you, remember that the airplane takes off against the wind, not with it.

—Henry Ford

~~~~~~~~~~~

Your success and happiness lie within you. External conditions are the accidents of life.

—Helen Keller

Do not go where the path may lead, go instead where there is no path and leave a trail.

—Ralph Waldo Emerson

Attitude is the paintbrush of the soul.

—Author Unknown

The word "listen" contains the same letters as the word "silent."

—Author Unknown

Take a chance! All life is a chance. The man who goes farthest is generally the one who is willing to do and dare.

—Dale Carnegie,
Philanthropist, Educator

Most of us die with our music still inside us.

—Oliver Wendell Holmes,
Author, Poet

How far you go in life depends on your being tender with the young, compassionate with the aged, sympathetic with the striving, and tolerant of

the weak and the strong. Because someday in life
you will have been all of these.

—George Washington Carver,
Agricultural Chemist,
Former Slave

———————

If you trust, you will be hurt, but if you don't trust,
you will never learn to love.

—Mahatma Gandhi

———————

Never give up, never give up, never, ever give up!

—Winston Churchill

———————

Lincoln was great, not because he was born in a log
cabin, but because he was able to get out of it.

—Hanoch McCarty,
Motivational Speaker,
Author

———————

We are what we repeatedly do. Excellence, then, is
not an act, but a habit.

—Aristotle

———————

Obstacles are those frightful things you see when
you take your eyes off the goal.

—Henry Ford

Here is the test to find whether your mission on earth is finished: if you're alive, it isn't.

—Richard Bach, Author

~~~~~~~~~~~

No one can make you feel inferior without your consent.

—Eleanor Roosevelt

~~~~~~~~~~~

When working with children what sustains us is an irrational hope.

—John Blaydes,
Educator, Author

~~~~~~~~~~~

Darkness cannot drive out darkness; only light can do that. Hate cannot drive out hate; only love can do that.

—Martin Luther King Jr.

~~~~~~~~~~~

The gains of education are never really lost; books may be burned and cities sacked, but truth, like the yearning for freedom, lives in the hearts of humble men.

—Franklin D. Roosevelt

When you do what you've always done, you get what you always got and you'll be where you've always been.

—Author Unknown

Poverty has many roots, but the taproot is ignorance.

—Lyndon B. Johnson

The future belongs to those that believe in the beauty of their dreams.

—Eleanor Roosevelt

There is no such thing as failure, only different outcomes.

—Author Unknown

If you think education is expensive, try ignorance.

—Derek Bok,
Harvard Professor, Author

I'm not concerned whether you failed, but if you are content with your failure.

—Abraham Lincoln

To read without reflecting is like eating without digesting.

—Edmund Burke,
British Statesman

———————

Discoveries big and small might have been made a lot sooner if someone had just said "You can" instead of "You can't."

—Author Unknown

———————

Happiness is a habit. Practice unhappy attitudes and become an unhappy person. Practice happy attitudes and learn that the habit becomes the person. Let positive thoughts become your habits.

—Author Unknown

———————

School is not preparation for life, but school is life.

—John Dewey,
Philosopher, Educator

———————

If you did your best yesterday, you've begun to die; if you're doing your best today, you're beginning to live!

—Northwest Sparkler,
Publication

How monotonous the sounds of the forest would be if the music came only from the top ten birds.

—Dan Bennett,
Comedian

~~~~~~~~~~~

Art is not the "icing on the cake," but the "yeast in the bread."

—Author Unknown

~~~~~~~~~~~

Education makes a people easy to lead, but difficult to drive; easy to govern, but impossible to enslave.

—Lord Brougham,
Lord Chancellor of England

~~~~~~~~~~~

"No" is a vitamin; it only makes me stronger!

—Author Unknown

~~~~~~~~~~~

Books were my pass to personal freedom. I learned to read at age three, and soon discovered there was a whole world to conquer that went beyond our farm in Mississippi.

—Oprah Winfrey

~~~~~~~~~~~

In happiness lies the joy of achievement and the thrill of creative effort.

—Franklin D. Roosevelt

Security is mostly a superstition. It does not exist in nature. Life is either a daring adventure or nothing.

—Helen Keller

He who has health has hope; and he who has hope has everything.

—Arabian Proverb

Triumph is just the extra "umph" added to the "try."

—Author Unknown

The greatest good is what we do for one another.

—Mother Teresa

People need love most when they deserve it least.

—Author Unknown

When you've exhausted all possibilities, remember this: you haven't!

—Robert Schuller,
Minister, Crystal Cathedral

Luck is a matter of preparation meeting opportunity.

—Oprah Winfrey

~~~~~~~~~~~

The best angle from which to approach any problem is the "try angle."

—Author Unknown

~~~~~~~~~~~

Poverty must not be a bar to learning and learning must offer an escape route from poverty.

—Lyndon B. Johnson

~~~~~~~~~~~

Most people are as happy as they make up their minds to be.

—Abraham Lincoln

~~~~~~~~~~~

I look for a day when education will be like the landscape, free for all. Beauty and truth should be free to everyone who has the capacity to absorb. The private school, the private library, the private art gallery, the exclusive college, have got to go. We want no excellence that is not for all.

—Elbert Hubbard,
Author, Publisher

Strongest minds are often those whom the noisy world hears least.

—Author Unknown

~~~~~~~~~~~~~

All things excellent are as difficult as they are rare.

—Benedict Spinoza,
Philosopher

~~~~~~~~~~~~~

We make a living by what we get, we make a life by what we give.

—Winston Churchill

~~~~~~~~~~~~~

When someone does something good, applaud! You will make two people happy.

—Samuel Goldwyn,
Movie Producer

~~~~~~~~~~~~~

It is not enough to be good if you have the ability to be better. It is not enough to be very good if you have the ability to be great.

—Albert Lee Cox,
Student, Grade 8

~~~~~~~~~~~~~

Perhaps I owe it to flowers to be a painter.

—Claude Monet

What would life be if we had no courage to attempt anything?

—Vincent Van Gogh

I am only one, but still I am one. I cannot do everything, but still I can do something. And because I cannot do everything I will not refuse to do the something that I can do.

—Helen Keller

There is no better place to be than where you are, and no better time than now to make a difference.

—Jim Kelly,
NFL Hall of Famer

The important thing is not so much that every child should be taught, as that every child should be given the wish to learn.

—Sir John Lubbock,
British Naturalist

All people smile in the same language.

—Author Unknown

Be yourself, try your best, and never be afraid to dream.

—Christa McAuliffe,
Teacher, Astronaut

*I believe in second chances, so I don't give
up on people or children. I know that if I have
a class full of kids, I want all of them to succeed.
Because of my own academic experiences, I don't
believe in quitting. I believe in finding solutions
to each and every problem. With all the chances
I was given, I am going to give my students as
many chances as they need to find themselves
as students.*

—Ennis Cosby, Teacher,
Son of Bill Cosby

*It is never too late to be what you might have
been.*

—George Eliot

*Keep your face to the sunshine and you cannot see
the shadow.*

—Helen Keller

*It's a funny thing about life. If you refuse to
accept anything but the best, you very often
get it.*

—Somerset Maugham,
Author

*Reading is the single most important social
factor in American life today. The more
you read, the more you know. The more
you know, the smarter you grow. The smarter
you grow, the longer you stay in school.
The longer you stay in school, the more
money you can earn. The more you earn, the
better your children will do in school, and the
longer you will live. So, if you hook a
child with reading, you influence not only
his future health and financial
circumstances, but also those of the next
generation.*

—Jim Trelease,
Educator, Author

*You are today where your thoughts have brought
you; you will be tomorrow where your thoughts
take you.*

—James Allen, Author

One man with courage is a majority.

—Thomas Jefferson

*Lord, grant that I may always desire more than I
can accomplish.*

—Michelangelo

You've got to get to the stage of life where going for it is more important than winning or losing.

—Arthur Ashe,
Tennis Champion

My only concern was to get home after a hard day's work.

—Rosa Parks,
Civil Rights Activist

Few will have the greatness to bend history itself, but each of us can work to change a small portion of events. It is from numberless acts of courage and belief that human history is shaped.

—Robert F. Kennedy

I know God will not give me anything I can't handle. I just wish that He didn't trust me so much.

—Mother Teresa

All our dreams can come true—if we have the courage to pursue them.

—Walt Disney

Let us have faith that right makes right; and in that faith let us to the end dare to do our duty as we understand it.

—Abraham Lincoln

———————

If you want to be happy, be.

—Tolstoy

———————

Hope is the feeling you have that the feeling you have isn't permanent.

—Jean Kerr, Writer,
Lyricist

———————

God does not want us to do extraordinary things; he wants us to do ordinary things extraordinarily well.

—Charles Gore, Bishop,
Theologian

———————

Happiness makes up in height for what it lacks in length.

—Robert Frost

———————

When we do the best that we can, we never know what miracle is wrought in our life, or in the life of another.

—Helen Keller

You can learn anything you need to learn to achieve any goal you set for yourself. There are no limits except the limits you place on your imagination.

—Brian Tracy,
Motivational Speaker,
Author

———————

So many of our dreams at first seem impossible, then they seem improbable and then, when we summon the will, they soon become inevitable.

—Christopher Reeve,
Actor

———————

We must not, in trying to think about how we can make a big difference, ignore the daily small differences we can make which, over time, add up to big differences that we often cannot foresee.

—Marion Wright Edelman,
Child Advocate, Author

———————

I am only one, but I am one. I cannot do everything, but I can do something; and what I can do, that I ought to do; and what I ought to do, by the grace of God I shall do.

—Edward Everett Hale,
Author, Teacher, Minister

*Some men see things as they are and say, "Why?" I
dream things that never were and say, "Why not?"*

—George Bernard Shaw

———————————

*In the pursuit of happiness half the world is on the
wrong scent. They think it consists in having and
getting, and in being served by others. Happiness is
really found in giving and in serving others.*

—Henry Drummond,
Author, Scientist,
Theologian

———————————

*The danger of the past was that men became
slaves. The danger of the future is that men may
become robots.*

—Erich Fromm,
Author, Holocaust Survivor

———————————

*What you get by achieving your goals is not as
important as what you become by achieving your
goals.*

—Zig Ziglar,
Author, Motivational Speaker

———————————

*Shoot for the moon. Even if you miss, you'll land
among the stars.*

—Author Unknown

Your job gives you authority. Your behavior earns you respect.

—Irwin Federman,
Businessman

~~~~~~~~~~~

Whoever undertakes to set himself up as judge in the field of truth and knowledge is shipwrecked by the laughter of the gods.

—Albert Einstein

~~~~~~~~~~~

Your past is important, but as important as that is, it is not nearly as important to your present as the way you see your future.

—Dr. Tony Campolo,
Minister

~~~~~~~~~~~

If you judge people you have no time to love them.

—Mother Teresa

~~~~~~~~~~~

We are the dwelling place of incredible opportunities. They live within us. With consciousness about who we are and what we are, with the awareness of the problems we're faced with, with a commitment not only to ourselves but to each other, we can make it work. We will make it work.

—John Denver,
Singer-Songwriter

When God made you, He threw away the mold.
There never has been or ever will be another person
just like you. So you are an original, a meticulously
designed instrument. That's great! But you will
never perform, live, or achieve above the value you
attribute to yourself.

—Author Unknown

THE ART OF TEACHING

It is the supreme art of the teacher to awaken joy in creative expression and knowledge.

—Albert Einstein

Nothing can replace that special relationship that gifted educators develop with their students. Popular culture has long celebrated other heroes— the athlete, the adventurer, the statesman—but except for the occasional tale of Mr. Chips, Annie Sullivan, or Jaime Escalante, teachers have not been celebrated in the same way. And classrooms have rarely been identified as the places where the greatest of human dramas unfold—the drama of igniting the human spirit, ennobling the human heart, and enriching the human experience.

—IBM TV Commercial

Whoever first coined the phrase, "You are the wind beneath my wings," most assuredly was reflecting on the sublime influence of a very special teacher.

—Author Unknown

Good teaching comes not from behind the desk but from behind the heart.

—Elizabeth Andrew,
Author

My heart is singing for joy this morning! A miracle has happened! The light of understanding has shone upon my little pupil's mind, and behold, all things are changed!

—Annie Sullivan,
Teacher of Helen Keller

Teachers usually have no way of knowing that they have made a difference in a child's life, even when they have made a dramatic one. But for children who are used to thinking of themselves as stupid or not worth talking to or deserving rape and beatings, a good teacher can provide an astonishing revelation. A good teacher can give a child at least a chance to feel, "She thinks I'm worth something, maybe I am." Good teachers put snags in the river of children passing by, and over the years, they redirect hundreds of lives.

—Tracy Kidder,
Pulitzer Prize-Winning Author

Teachers leave footprints on the souls of children.

—Author Unknown

Teaching is the profession that teaches all the other professions.

—Author Unknown

The whole art of teaching is only the art of awakening the natural curiosity of young minds for the purpose of satisfying it afterwards.

—Author Unknown

If we don't model what we teach, we are teaching something else.

—Abraham Maslow,
        Founder of Humanistic
        Psychology

————————

Reading helps us grow, head and heart. It gets children ready for school and helps them do better once they get there. It's a special time for children to be close to grown-ups who care for them, a wonderful way to feel loved.

—Barbara Bush,
        Former First Lady

————————

Good teaching is loving and listening, sharing and supporting. It is being passionately human. That is the point at which a good teacher begins.

—Author Unknown

————————

Tribute to a teacher: To a special person in my life. Thank you for reaching deep into the corners of my being and seeing a part of me I did not know existed and others never saw. Thank you for your faith in my abilities and my future even when I did not believe. Thank you for sharing a part of your humanity and for the spark that glows warmly inside me. Thank you. Your influence is etched on my soul forever.

—Dr. Susan Parks,
        School Administrator

*Learning and teaching are two sides of the
same coin. Both rely on a sense of timing,
a state of readiness, a heightened sensibility,
which enables one to see or say or think something
not seen or said or thought before. Readiness is
achieved in different ways, depending upon
what there is to be learned. Sometimes it
requires painful and protracted effort—thinking,
reading, watching, writing, talking, doing.
Other times it is attained effortlessly, almost
inadvertently. Either way, timing is critical.
Knowing how to learn or how to teach is
essentially knowing when to press and when to
wait. Styles of learning and teaching are
characterized by their mix of pressure and
patience. Thorough education will expose teachers
and students to a range of styles so that they
come to know their own.*

—Bob McCarthy, Principal,
Brookline High School,
Brookline, MA

---

*If a doctor, lawyer, or dentist had 40 people in their
office at one time, all of whom had different needs,
and some of whom didn't want to be there and
were causing trouble, and the doctor, lawyer, or
dentist, without assistance, had to treat them all
with professional excellence for nine months, then
he might have some conception of the classroom
teacher's job.*

—Donald D. Quinn,
Author

Education: That which discloses to the wise and disguises from the foolish their lack of understanding.

—Ambrose Bierce,
Writer, Humorist

———————————

Today society asks more of educators than ever before. You are required to be social workers, computer experts, juvenile officers, mediators, researchers, business partners, interdisciplinary team members, and chemical dependency counselors. You must provide for children who don't speak English; who are gifted learners, visual learners, kinesthetic learners, voracious learners, and reluctant learners; who are emotionally disturbed, hungry, and homeless. We ask you to teach children how to drive, get along with others, balance a checkbook, make healthy choices, use new technologies— and, yes, how to read, write, and do arithmetic.

—Author Unknown

———————————

Socrates didn't have an overhead projector. He asked questions that bothered people and 3,500 years later people are still talking about him.

—Hanoch McCarty,
Motivational Speaker,
Author

The secret of teaching is to appear to have known
all your life what you learned this afternoon.

—Author Unknown

Death is silent; education is noisy.

—Author Unknown

To be a teacher in the right sense is to be
a learner. I am not a teacher, only a fellow
student.

—Kierkegaard

Every child, regardless of the disguise, knows what
he or she is not. We must teach every child what he
or she can be.

—Author Unknown

Teaching is the real world. It's like making love
standing up in a hammock—you need balance,
grace, and a hell of a lot of perseverance.

—Hanoch McCarty,
Motivational Speaker,
Author

Children absorb our lessons, and then time and experience help knit them together. Thought is a process, not an event.

—Author Unknown

Sometimes the difference between being ordinary and extraordinary resides in the moment at which passion enters what we teach and how.

—Author Unknown

However hard we may preach, it is by example that we teach.

—Old Saying

Our neighborhoods represent the best and last frontier in our collaborative efforts to advocate for and improve the lives of children. It is within the structure of neighborhoods that children develop, incorporate values, and eventually learn the skills necessary for responsible citizenship.

—Charles DeLeo, Author

If you would thoroughly know anything, teach it to others.

—Tyron Edwards, Author

It's not that we make a difference—we make the difference for the future.

—Bob Harris, Teacher

~~~~~~~~~~

Students need to know that you care before they care what you know.

—Author Unknown

~~~~~~~~~~

The home environment is a most powerful factor in determining the level of school achievement of students, student interest in learning, and the number of years of schooling the children will receive. It accounts for more of the student's motivation in learning than does the school curriculum or the quality of instruction in our schools.

—Benjamin Bloom,
Educational Psychologist

~~~~~~~~~~

When they need to speak, you listen; when they need to listen, you speak; when they need to question, you answer; and when they need to answer, you question. Knowing when is just a part of what makes you a great teacher!

—Author Unknown

I've come to the frightening conclusion that I am the decisive element in the classroom. It is my personal approach that creates the climate. It is my daily mood that creates the weather. As a teacher, I possess a tremendous power to make a child's life miserable or joyous. I can be a tool of torture or an instrument of inspiration.

—Haim Ginott,
Teacher, Author

~~~~~~~~~~

Teachers inspire dreams, shape lives, and give us hope for the future.

—Author Unknown

~~~~~~~~~~

All students can learn and succeed, but not on the same day in the same way.

—William G. Spady,
Educational Theorist

~~~~~~~~~~

Remember: A student's greatest thinking will come from his or her ability to break away—not to conform.

—Author Unknown

~~~~~~~~~~

Who dares to teach must never cease to learn.

—John Cotton Dana,
Author

If all children had a safe harbor, none would be at risk.

—Author Unknown

————————

The good teacher is someone who can understand those not very good at explaining and explain it to those not very good at understanding.

—W. A. Palmer, Author

————————

As teachers we have a chance to leave our thumbprint on children's lives. Let that thumbprint be that we did make a difference! Let our goal as teachers be to reach that unreachable child. Let us make that our challenge! Just one unreachable child! Is there anything more noble or honorable than making a difference in one child's life? Teachers can and do make a difference!

—John Blaydes,
  Motivational Speaker, Author

————————

The most significant word in teacher is "each."

—Robert DeBruyn,
  Author

————————

No calling in society is more demanding than teaching; no calling in our society is more selfless than teaching; and no calling is more central to the vitality of a democracy than teaching.

—Roger Mudd,
  News Commentator

Teachers affect eternity; they can never tell where their influence stops.

> —Henry Adams,
> Historian

We expect teachers to handle teenage pregnancy, substance abuse, and the failings of the family. Then we expect them to educate our children.

> —John Sculley,
> Businessman

Education is not filling a pail but the lighting of a fire.

> —William Butler Yeats

Good teaching is one-fourth preparation and three-fourths theater.

> —Gail Godwin, Novelist

Modern cynics and skeptics see no harm in paying those to whom we entrust the minds of their children a smaller wage than is paid to those to whom they entrust the care of their plumbing.

> —John F. Kennedy

Never say "I can't"; say "Teach me how."

> —Author Unknown

He that teaches himself hath a fool for a master.

—Benjamin Franklin

————————

Teachers are the important link to the future and the world of knowledge and self-esteem for children. We need to strengthen the chain that brings us together in a worthwhile and noble cause—teaching! Let us continue to strengthen the chain that brings us together. We are a team, but we are only as strong as our weakest link!

—John Blaydes,
Motivational Speaker, Author

————————

The mediocre teacher tells. The good teacher explains. The superior teacher demonstrates. The great teacher inspires.

—William Arthur Ward,
Author

————————

In a completely rational society, the best of us would aspire to be teachers and the rest of us would have to settle for something less, because passing civilization along from one generation to the next ought to be the highest honor and the highest responsibility anyone could have.

—Lee Iaccoca,
Businessman, Author

To teach is to transform by informing, to develop a zest for lifelong learning, to help pupils become students—mature independent learners, architects of an exciting, challenging future. Teaching at its best is a kind of communion, a meeting and a merging of the minds.

—Edgar Dale, Author

Thank you for exemplifying the best of the education profession. You give students hope and the means to fulfill their aspirations as you guide, nourish, encourage, discipline, and love them. The young minds that you mold are our leaders of tomorrow. You are making a difference in preparing them for the challenges to come by encouraging them to make a lifelong commitment to learning.

—Gene Wilhoit,
Kentucky State
Commissioner of Education

The master teacher that lurks within each of us is likelier to burst forth within the intellectual atmosphere that collegiality can create.

—Author Unknown

*It has long been clear to me that teaching
is at once the most difficult and the most
honorable of professions. We have all been
touched by the example, guidance, and motivation
of a teacher whose often-reluctant pupil we
were. We can recall a moment of insight or truth
when caught in the act of learning. None of us may
owe larger debts for whatever we may have
become, for whatever we may have been able to
accomplish, than we owe to teachers in our past
lives whose total devotion to young people and
their discipline has been their chief reward and the
reason we honor teachers and the teaching
profession.*

—William Friday, Author

*As you well know, there are few professions
as challenging as teaching. Families, businesses,
and communities in general entrust teachers with
the weighty task of preparing students to be
lifelong learners, productive workers, and
responsible citizens. The increasing complexity of
the world, with burdensome social issues and
shifting economic demands, makes the work more
difficult than ever before. Yet, for those like you
who choose the profession and dedicate yourselves
to doing it well, the rewards make the journey
worthwhile.*

—Peter McWalters,
Rhode Island State
Commissioner of
Education

Feed a man a fish and you've fed him for a day. Teach a man to fish and you've fed him for a lifetime.

—Old Saying

Most people believe that all that is required of teachers is knowledge of the subject matter. We know much better. We have seen many experts in the content who cannot teach. The world is full of people who can do, but can't teach. We can.

—Albert Foshay, Teacher

You quietly get the job done, and you do so with incredible dedication, perseverance, and dignity in an environment of steadily diminishing resources and escalating criticism of schools. Why do you do it? I believe the answer is very simple. You love children. You want to help give children the best possible start in life.

—Nancy Keenan,
Montana State
Superintendent of Education

The task of the best teacher is to balance the difficult juggling act of becoming vitally, vigorously, creatively, energetically, and inspiringly unnecessary.

—Gerald O. Grow,
Author

As adults, when we think back to our years in school, we remember teachers, not instructional methods and techniques. We remember the teachers who saw something special in us and made a connection, planting those cherished memories and good feelings that continue to live within us wherever we are or whatever we've become.

—John Blaydes,
Motivational Speaker, Author

The role of teacher remains the highest calling of a free people. To the teacher our nation entrusts her most precious resource, her children, and asks that they be prepared in all their glorious diversity, to face the rigors of individual participation in a democratic society.

—Shirley Hufstedler,
Former U.S. Secretary
of Education

But let us never forget that the true heroes of our society are not to be found on a movie screen or football field. They are to be found in our classrooms.

—Elizabeth Dole,
U. S. Senator

I hear and I forget; I see and I remember; I do and I understand.

—Chinese Proverb

One looks back with appreciation to the brilliant
teachers, but with gratitude to those who touched
our human feelings.

—Carl Jung

Books are the carriers of civilization. Without
books, history is silent, literature dumb, science
crippled, thought and speculation at a standstill.

—Barbara Tuchman,
Pulitzer Prize-Winning Author

"Tell me what you read and I'll tell you who you
are" is true enough, but I'd know you better if you
told me what you reread.

—Francois Mauriac,
Nobel Prize-Winning Author

A great teacher never strives to explain his vision—he
simply invites you to stand beside him and see for
yourself.

—Rev. R. Inman, Author

Learning is finding out what you already know. Doing
is demonstrating that you know it. Teaching is
reminding others that they know it just as well as you.

—Author Unknown

You are all learners, doers, teachers.

—Richard Bach, Author

———————

I touch the future. I teach.

—Christa McAuliffe,
Teacher, Astronaut

CHILDREN

Mankind owes to the child
the best it has to give.

—United Nations
Declaration

The greatest gifts you can give your children are the roots of responsibility and the wings of independence.

—Dennis Waitley,
Motivational Speaker, Author

———————————

Children need love especially when they don't deserve it.

—Harold S. Hulbert,
Author

———————————

We worry about what a child will be tomorrow, yet we forget that he is somebody today.

—Stacia Tauscher,
Mother

———————————

Children are like sponges, they absorb all your energy, but give them a squeeze and you'll get it all back.

—Author Unknown

———————————

What we want for your children . . . we should want for their teachers; that schools be places of learning for both of them, and that such learning be suffused with excitement, engagement, passion, challenge, creativity and joy.

—Andy Hargreaves,
Educator, Author

~~~~~~~~~~

Of course class size is important! You have to find the child to teach the child!

—Author Unknown

~~~~~~~~~~

I have found that the best way to give advice to your children is to find out what they want and then advise them to do it.

—Harry S. Truman

~~~~~~~~~~

To show a child what once delighted you, to find the child's delight added to your own—this is happiness.

—J. B. Priestly,
Author, Playwright

~~~~~~~~~~

In the traditional method the child must say something that he has merely learned. There is all the difference in the world between having something to say and having to say something.

—John Dewey,
Educator, Philosopher

With children, there is sometimes no substitute for parental time periods of unhurried, undivided attention. Often, even the best parents forget that need, or develop lifestyles which provide no room for it. We find ourselves so problem-oriented as parents that we spend most of our time with our children as troubleshooters. When our child needs our help, whether to tie his shoe or to get a driver's license, we address the problem, help as best we can, and move on. But often there is no particular thing our children need from us; what they need is just for us to be there.

—Dr. Charles Paul Conn,
Author, Psychologist

What you think of me, I will think of me. What I think of me, I will be.

—Author Unknown

Children are the living messages we send to a time we will not see.

—Neil Postman,
Technologist, Author

All children are gifted; some just open their packages earlier than others.

—Michael Carr, Author

Yet we will make no substantial, lasting improvement, I am convinced, until we realize that the roots of our students' deficiencies lie in their earliest years—in the family lives, not in our classrooms. It is not better curricula that American students need most; it is better childhoods.

>—Sam Salva,
>NAESP Executive Director

By being frequently in the company of children, we may learn to recapture the will to laugh and the art of laughing at will.

>—Rabbi Julius Gordon

I have often wondered about two things. First, why high school kids almost invariably hate the books they are assigned to read by their English teachers, and second, why English teachers almost invariably hate the books students read in their spare time. Something seems very wrong with such a situation. There is a bridge out here, and the ferry service is uncertain at best.

>—Stephen King, Novelist

When I was a boy of fourteen, my father was so ignorant I could hardly stand to have the old man around. But when I got to be twenty-one, I was astonished at how much the old man had learned in seven years.

>—Mark Twain

*Think before you speak. Read before you think.
This will give you something to think about that
you didn't make up yourself—a wise move at any
age, but most especially at seventeen, when you are
at the greatest danger of coming to annoying
conclusions.*

—Fran Liebowitz, Author

~~~~~~~~~~

*What we want is to see the child in pursuit of
knowledge, and not knowledge in pursuit of the
child.*

—George Bernard Shaw

~~~~~~~~~~

*Children who are treated as if they are uneducable
almost invariably become uneducable.*

—Kenneth B. Clark,
Educator, Social Activist

~~~~~~~~~~

*No one has yet fully realized the wealth of
sympathy, kindness, and generosity hidden in the
soul of a child. The effort of every true education
should be to unlock that treasure.*

—Emma Goldman,
Author, Social Activist

~~~~~~~~~~

*It is unreasonable to expect a child to listen to your
advice and ignore your example.*

—Author Unknown

The young do not know enough to be prudent, and therefore they attempt the impossible—and achieve it, generation after generation.

—Pearl Buck, Author,
Missionary in China

Schools are like a jigsaw puzzle. Each edge piece of a puzzle interlocks with two others to form the puzzle's framework and give structure and support to the puzzle as a whole. Each piece has a unique design and cut that ensures just the right place to fit within the puzzle. Each morning, staff members form the edge pieces that interlock to create a safe environment and give support to one another and the whole. Each morning, they provide just the "right place" for every student to fit safely and securely. The staff members are strength and stability, and like the edge pieces, they do not stand alone in this responsibility. There are always others to support and assist, ensuring that every student has a place.

—Karen Hegeman,
Author

The mind of a child is fascinating, for it looks on old things with new eyes.

—F. Scott Fitzgerald

What should not be heard by little ears should not be said by big mouths.

—Author Unknown

An ounce of praise can accomplish more than a ton of fault finding. And if one looks for it, something worthy of praise can be found in every child.

—John Drescher, Author

———————————

I will teach things that are not in books. For instance, I believe that children will be better students if they like each other and themselves better.

—Ennis Cosby, Teacher,
Son of Bill Cosby

———————————

If there is anything we wish to change in the child, we should first examine it and see whether it is not something that could better be changed in ourselves.

—Carl Jung

———————————

If you want your children to keep their feet on the ground, put some responsibility on their shoulders.

—Abigail Van Buren,
Newspaper Columnist

———————————

Cherishing children is the mark of a civilized society.

—Joan Ganz Cooney,
Founder, Children's
Television Workshop
(Sesame Street)

The best security blanket a child can have is parents who respect each other.

> —Jan Blaustone,
> Substitute Teacher, Author

~~~~~~~~~~

Let us unite in the mightiest, the biggest arms race in history, a race to put our arms around our children, around all our children. Let us embrace them with love, courage, hope, respect, education, opportunity, and let the imperatives of our arms race fix our national priorities so that no child in America shall in effect be denied the right to dream.

> —Eugene Lang,
> Philanthropist

~~~~~~~~~~

The lesson you teach today is not confined to the walls of your classroom. Once it is implanted in the heart and mind of a child, it can change the world.

> —Author Unknown

~~~~~~~~~~

The least likely child may be the one you reach today. Yesterday you may have been discouraged, but today you see something you didn't see before. Maybe this is what yesterdays are for.

> —Author Unknown

Each second we live is a new and unique moment of the universe, a moment that never was before and will never be again. And what do we teach our children in school? We teach them that two and two make four and that Paris is the capital of France. When will we also teach them what they are? We should say to each of them . . . "Do you know what you are? You are a marvel. You are unique. In all of the world there is no other child exactly like you. In the millions of years that have passed there has never been another child like you. And look at your body . . . what a wonder it is! You may become a Shakespeare, a Michelangelo, a Beethoven. You have the capacity for anything. Yes, you are a marvel. And when you grow up, can you then harm another who is, like you, a marvel? You must cherish one another. You must work; we all must work to make this world worthy of its children. The love of one's country is a natural thing, but why should love stop at the border? We are all leaves of a tree and the tree is humanity."

—Pablo Cassals, Cellist

A child is a person who is going to carry on what you have started. He is going to move in and take over your church, schools, universities, and corporations. The fate of humanity is in his hands.

—Abraham Lincoln

There is always a moment in a child's life when the door opens and lets the future in.

—Graham Greene, Author

Children have more need of models than of critics.

—Carolyn Coats, Author

Children need your presence more than they need your presents.

—Rev. Jesse Jackson

Within even the reluctant student there is a small part that wants desperately to learn. The strength of the desire is determined by the teacher's belief in him or her.

—Author Unknown

Be careful what you say around children. They are like blotters: They soak it all in and get it all backward.

—Author Unknown

Life affords no greater responsibility, no greater privilege, than the raising of the next generation.

—C. Everett Koop,
Former U.S. Surgeon
General

We need 4 hugs a day for survival. We need 8 hugs a day for maintenance. We need 12 hugs a day for growth.

—Virginia Satir,
Family Therapist, Author

When I approach a child, he inspires in me two sentiments: tenderness for what he is, and respect for what he may become.

—Louis Pasteur

The greatest natural resource that any country can have is its children.

—Danny Kaye,
Actor, Comedian

Smile at each other, smile at your wife, smile at your husband, smile at your children, smile at each other—it doesn't matter who it is—and that will help you to grow up in greater love for each other.

—Mother Teresa

4
CHARACTER

I have a dream that my four little children will one day live in a nation where they will not be judged by the color of their skin, but by the content of their character.

—*Martin Luther King Jr.*

Character is what you do when no one is looking.

>   —Author Unknown

———————————

Try not to become a man of success but rather a man of value.

>   —Albert Einstein

———————————

What lies behind us and what lies before us are tiny matters compared to what lies within us.

>   —William Morrow,
>   Philosopher, Poet

———————————

Be more concerned with your character than your reputation, because your character is what you really are, while your reputation is merely what others think you are.

>   —John Wooden,
>   Basketball Coach

———————————

Character is ultimately who we are expressed in action, in how we live, in what we do, and so the children around us know: they absorb and take stock of what they observe, namely us,—we adults living and doing things in a certain spirit, getting on with one another in various ways. Our children add up, imitate, file away what they've observed and so very often later fall in line with the particular moral

counsel me wittingly or quite unself-consciously
have offered them.

—Robert Coles,
    Child Psychiatrist, Author

~~~~~~~~~~~~~

*We judge ourselves by what we are capable of
doing; others judge us by what we have done.*

—Jack Dempsey, Boxer

~~~~~~~~~~~~~

*If you want to take your mission in life to the next
level, if you're stuck and you don't know how to
rise, don't look outside yourself. Look inside. Don't
let your fears keep you mired in the crowd. Abolish
your fears and raise your commitment level to the
point of no return, and I guarantee you that the
Champion Within will burst forth to propel you
toward victory.*

—Bruce Jenner,
    Olympic Gold Medalist

~~~~~~~~~~~~~

*I believe life is constantly testing us for our level of
commitment, and life's greatest rewards are reserved
for those who demonstrate a never-ending
commitment to act until they achieve. This level of
resolve can move mountains, but it must be constant
and consistent. As simplistic as this may sound, it is
still the common denominator separating those who
live their dreams from those who live in regret.*

—Anthony Robbins,
    Motivational Speaker, Author

The test of courage comes when we are in the minority; the test of tolerance comes when we are in the majority.

—Ralph W. Stockman,
Author

Respect. Learning how to respect begins with learning how to listen. Listening begins with being tolerant of what we hear. Learning tolerance teaches us how to understand. Understanding allows us to learn how to care. Caring means we've learned how to respect. Just like a toddler, we take one step at a time. Just like a puzzle, we find one piece at a time. Just like building a bridge, we connect one section at a time. So learning respect is just how I said, it's one step, one piece, one section at a time, but the finished product can make the world safe from all the wars and destruction of human kind. Because we have listened, because we were tolerant, because we understood, because we cared, we learned to respect and we created a world to care for all of mankind.

—Andrew Ter Bush,
Student, Age 10

A champion is one who gets up when he can't.

—Jack Dempsey, Boxer

If you stand for nothing, you'll fall for anything.

—Author Unknown

Anything that a child should do and can do, and we do for them, takes away an opportunity to learn responsibility.

—Gene Bedley,
Educator, Author

————————

Let us rise up and be thankful, for if we didn't learn a lot today, at least we learned a little, and if we didn't learn a little, at least we didn't get sick, and if we got sick, at least we didn't die. So, let us all be thankful.

—Buddha

————————

Friendship is like a bank account. You can't continue to draw on it without making deposits.

—Author Unknown

————————

Listen to your enemies; they tell you your faults.

—Benjamin Franklin

————————

Commitment is something that if you have it, nothing else matters; but if you don't have it, then nothing else matters very much either.

—Sir James Barrie,
Author of Peter Pan

Perhaps the most valuable result of all education is the ability to make yourself do the thing you have to do, when it ought to be done, whether you like it or not.

—Thomas Henry Huxley,
Philosopher, Scientist

The power to hold on in spite of everything, the power to endure—this is the winner's quality. Persistence is the ability to face defeat again and again without giving up—to push on in the face of great difficulty, knowing that victory can be yours. Persistence means taking pain to overcome every obstacle, and to do what's necessary to reach your goals.

—Author Unknown

Where I was born and where and how I have lived is unimportant. It is what I have done with where I have been that should be of interest.

—Georgia O'Keeffe,
Artist

The more ignorant you are the quicker you fight.

—Will Rogers, Comedian

The will to win is worth nothing unless you have the will to prepare.

—Inscription at U.S. Air
Force Academy

Happiness is not a state to arrive at, but a manner
of traveling.

—Margaret Lee Runbeck,
Author

Don't pretend to be what you don't intend to be.
Many people fear nothing more terribly than to
take a position, which stands out sharply and
clearly from the prevailing opinion. The tendency of
most is to adopt a view that is so ambiguous that it
will include everything and so popular that it will
include everybody. Not a few people who cherish
lofty and noble ideals, hide them under a bushel for
fear of being called different.

—Martin Luther King Jr.

Associate with men of good quality, if you esteem
your own reputation, for it is better to be alone
than in bad company.

—George Washington

Parents can only give good advice or put [children]
on the right paths, but the final forming of a
person's character lies in their own hands.

—Anne Frank, Diarist

Every man has three characters: that which he exhibits,
that which he has, and that which he thinks he has.

—Alphonse Karr,
French Journalist, Novelist

You can't always judge a book by its cover, but it's still the first thing you see.

> —Author Unknown

Tact: the ability to describe others as they see themselves.

> —Abraham Lincoln

Loyalty, very simply, is the desire to help other people become successful.

> —Zig Ziglar,
> Motivational Speaker, Author

We are what we pretend to be, so we must be careful about what we pretend to be.

> —Kurt Vonnegut, Author

Far and away the best prize that life offers is the chance to work hard at work that is worth doing.

> —Theodore Roosevelt

Even the woodpecker owes his success to the fact that he uses his head, and keeps pecking away until he finishes the job he starts.

> —Coleman Cox, Author

Your attitude speaks so loudly, I can't hear what you are saying!

—Peter Drucker, Author

You can't shake hands with clenched fists.

—Golda Meir,
Former Prime Minister of Israel

Only the open gate can receive visitors. Only the open hand can receive gifts. Only the open mind can receive wisdom. Only the open heart can receive love.

—Joan Walsh Anglund,
Children's Author/Illustrator

When in doubt, tell the truth.

—Mark Twain

Whatever you are, be a good one.

—Abraham Lincoln

Tact is the art of making a point without making an enemy.

—Howard Newton,
Author

For the ignorant, old age is a winter; for the learned it is a harvest.

—Jewish Proverb

———————————

Rationalize equals rational lies.

—Millard MacAdam,
Educator, Author

———————————

Keep away from people who try to belittle your ambitions. Small people always do that, but the really great make you feel that you, too, can become great.

—Mark Twain

———————————

To refuse praise is to seek praise twice.

—Francois de La Rochefoucald,
French Author

———————————

Character consists of what you do on the third and fourth tries.

—James Michener,
Novelist

In ninth grade my dream was to beat my brother Larry at a game of one-on-one. He'd beat me every time and I'd get mad. In tenth grade my dream was to make the varsity team, but I didn't and I had to play junior varsity all year. When I look back on these experiences, I know they must have built determination in me.

—Michael Jordan,
Basketball Player

Leadership is a potent combination of strategy and character. But if you must be without one, be without the strategy.

—General Norman Schwarzkopf

Patience is a virtue that carries a lot of wait.

—Author Unknown

Be bold in what you stand for and careful in what you fall for.

—Ruth Boorstin, Author

Don't laugh at a youth for his affectations; he is only trying on one face after another to find a face of his own.

—Logan Pearsall Smith,
Essayist

One of the best ways to measure people is to watch the way they behave when something free is offered.

—Ann Landers,
Newspaper Columnist

The reputation of a thousand years
may be determined by the conduct of
one hour.

—Japanese Proverb

In great matters men show themselves as they wish to be seen; in small matters, as they are.

—Gamaliel Bradford,
Poet

Nearly all men can stand adversity, but if
you want to test a man's character, give
him power.

—Abraham Lincoln

The foundations of character are built not by
lecture, but by bricks of good example, laid
day by day.

—Leo Blessing, Author

Good character is more to be praised than outstanding talent. Most talents are, to some extent, a gift. Good character, by contrast, is not given to us. We have to build it piece by piece—by thought, choice, courage, and determination.

—John Luther, Author

~~~~~~~~~~

Courage is very important. Like a muscle, it is strengthened by use.

—Ruth Gordon, Actress

~~~~~~~~~~

The measure of a man's real character is what he would do if he knew he never would be found out.

—Lord Thomas B. Macaulay, Essayist

~~~~~~~~~~

The will is more important than the skill when it comes to scaling a wall.

—Robert Schuller, Minister

~~~~~~~~~~

Honesty is the first chapter in the book of wisdom.

—Thomas Jefferson

~~~~~~~~~~

The wishbone will never replace the backbone.

—Will Henry, Author

Character cannot be developed in ease and quiet. Only through experience of trial and suffering can the soul be strengthened, ambition inspired, and success achieved.

—Helen Keller

Courage is fear holding on a minute longer.

—General George S. Patton

Enthusiasm is the electric current that keeps the engine of life going at top speed. Enthusiasm is the very propeller of progress.

—B. C. Forbes, Publisher

Courage is not the absence of fear; rather it is the ability to take action in the face of fear.

—Ambrose Redmoon,
New Age Writer

Reputation is that which people are believed to be; character is that which people are.

—Napoleon Hill,
Motivational Speaker,
Author

Tact is the ability to make a person see the lightning without letting him feel the bolt.

—Orlando A. Battista,
Author

———————————————

Patience is the ability to count down before blasting off.

—Author Unknown

———————————————

Enthusiasm and joy are Siamese twins—it's hard to find one without the other.

—Author Unknown

MANAGING CHANGE

Change is mandatory;
growth is optional.

—*Michael Fullan, Author,*
Professor of Education

Change is an inevitable journey. All things are constantly changing, transforming, becoming something different. Guiding change so that it is successful is what leadership is all about. Indeed, the measure of a leader may well be her or his capacity to understand and deal successfully with change—to stimulate it, shape it, guide it, manage it, and keep it going in the right direction.

—California School
Leadership Academy

The world we have created is a product of our thinking; it cannot be changed without changing our thinking.

—Albert Einstein

If in the last few years, you haven't discarded a major opinion or acquired a new one, check your pulse, you may be dead.

—Gelett Burgess,
Humorist, Poet

Change is the law of life. And those who look only to the past or the present are certain to miss the future.

—John F. Kennedy

In times of change, learners inherit the earth, while the learned find themselves beautifully equipped to deal with a world that no longer exists.

—Eric Hoffer, Philosopher

When your views on the world and your intellect are being challenged and you begin to feel uncomfortable because of a contradiction you've detected that is threatening your current model of the world or some aspect of it, pay attention. You are about to learn something. This discomfort and intellectual conflict is when learning is taking place.

—William Drury, Author

Everyone thinks of changing the world, but no one thinks of changing himself.

—Leo Tolstoy

You are what you are and where you are because of what has gone into your mind; you change what you are and where you are by changing what goes into your mind.

—Zig Ziglar, Author,
Motivational Speaker

To exist is to change, to change is to mature, to mature is to go on creating oneself endlessly.

—Henri Bergson,
Philosopher, Author

Seek the rapids, not the calm of the lake. Take the calm to reflect and prepare for the rapids. If we face permanent white water, we will see the need for and experience change.

—Peter Vaille, Author

———————

People who say it cannot be done should not interrupt those of us who are doing it.

—George Bernard Shaw

———————

Americans always do the right thing after they try everything else first.

—Winston Churchill

———————

Sometimes only a change of viewpoint is needed to convert a tiresome duty into an interesting opportunity.

—Alberta Flanders,
Author

———————

Never doubt that a small group of thoughtful committed citizens can change the world. Indeed, it is the only thing that ever has.

—Margaret Mead,
Anthropologist

Things remain the same because it is impossible to change very much without changing most of everything.

> —Ted Sizer, Educator,
> Author

~~~~~~~~~~~

Success is a journey, not a destination.

> —Author Unknown

~~~~~~~~~~~

Nothing in the world is so powerful as an idea whose time has come.

> —Victor Hugo

~~~~~~~~~~~

A journey of a thousand miles must begin with a single step.

> —Chinese proverb

~~~~~~~~~~~

If you have always done it that way, it is probably wrong.

> —Charles Kettering,
> Engineer, Businessman

~~~~~~~~~~~

Many schools resist change while others avidly seek it. If we do not want our schools to atrophy and die, we need educational leaders who can bring about progress by daring to be change managers.

> —Jon Andreas, Author

Not doing more than the average is what keeps the average down.

—William M. Winans,
Author

~~~~~~~~~

The world changes faster than the people in it.

—Author Unknown

~~~~~~~~~

As things are now, education is so cluttered and tangled up with a thousand senseless notions and stupidities, that the task of reformation is almost a superhuman one. It is entirely a task of taking away and reducing—not one of adding to, or explaining. It is the task of the sculptor, who cuts the superfluous marble off, rather than that of the wax-workman who lays on the stuff thicker and thicker.

—Walt Whitman

~~~~~~~~~

A ship in port is safe, but that's not what ships are built for.

—Navy Admiral Grace Hopper

~~~~~~~~~

Positive school change is built on common dreams, common concern, common aspirations, common trust, and common sense!

—Michael Hoy, Author

*Those individuals and organizations that are most
effective do not experience fewer problems, less
stressful situations, and greater fortune—they just
deal with them differently.*

> —Michael Fullan, Author,
> Professor of Education

----

*The problem is not that there are problems. The
problem is expecting otherwise and thinking that
having problems is a problem.*

> —Theodore Rubin,
> Author

----

*Probably the most dramatic metaphor for change as
the watchword of our time is the experience of the
Russian Cosmonaut Krikalev, who left Leningrad for
a 313-day journey in space in 1991. Almost a year
later he returned to a city no longer on the map
and a country that no longer existed.*

> —Author Unknown

----

*Great changes require administrative support and
necessary resources. Without these two elements
the potential will die a slow death and the old
negative patterns will return.*

> —Author Unknown

Some people grin and bear it. Others smile and change it.

—Author Unknown

———————

Go to the people. Learn from them. Love them. Start with what they know. Build on what they have. And the best leaders, when their task is accomplished, and their work is done, the people will remark: we have done it ourselves.

—Chinese Proverb

———————

We do not really see through our eyes and hear through our ears, but through our beliefs. To put our beliefs on hold is to cease to exist as ourselves for a moment—and that is not easy. It is painful as well, because it means turning yourself inside out, giving up your own sense of who you are, and being willing to see yourself in the unflattering light of another's angry gaze. It is not easy, but it is the only way to learn what it might feel like to be someone else and the only way to start a dialogue.

—Lisa D. Delpit,
Educator, Author

Change is like a trapeze—you've got to let go before you grab hold and timing is everything.

—Terrence Deal,
Educator, Author

Changing too much too quickly may cause damage or leave valuable things behind. For any organization to progress in a healthy way, there must be a careful balancing of the wisdom of the past and the needs of the future. For change to be a positive force for good, it must be managed.

—Woodrow Hughes,
University Professor of Education

Lord, where we are wrong, make us willing to change; where we are right, make us easy to live with.

—Rev. Peter Marshall,
U.S. Senate Chaplain, Author

The only thing that can change you from where you are now to where you'll be five years from now are the books you read, the people you meet, and the dreams you dream.

—Lou Holtz, Football Coach

The climate of change that defines turn-of-the-century life is with us to stay. And while change of this magnitude demands greater adaptability and a commitment to lifelong learning, it also promises huge opportunity for those who know where and how to look for it.

—*Lowell Milken,*
Philantropist, Educational Reformer

If you come to comfort the disturbed, you will surely disturb the comfortable.

—*Author Unknown*

It's not so much that we're afraid of change or so in love with the old ways, but it's that place in between that we fear. It's like being in between trapezes. It's Linus when his blanket is in the dryer. There's nothing to hold onto.

—*Marilyn Ferguson,*
Psychologist, Author

A vision without a plan is only a dream.

—*Joel Barker,*
Author, Futurist

Vision is the capacity to create and communicate a view of a desired state of affairs that induces commitment among those working in the organization.

—Thomas Sergiovani,
Author

———————————

Make sustained rapid improvement a way of life.

—Brian Joiner, Author

———————————

Nothing is so fatiguing as the eternal hanging on of an uncompleted task.

—William James,
Philosopher, Psychologist

———————————

There is nothing wrong in change if it is in the right direction. To improve is to change, so to be perfect is to have changed often.

—Winston Churchill

———————————

Start by doing what's necessary; then do what's possible; and suddenly you are doing the impossible.

—St. Francis of Assisi

Learning to lead is, on one level, learning to manage change. . . . A leader imposes (in the most positive sense of the word) his philosophy on the organization, creating or re-creating its culture. The organization then acts on that philosophy, carries out the mission, and the culture takes on a life of its own, becomes more cause than effect. But, unless the leader continues to evolve, to adapt and adjust to external changes, the organization will sooner or later fall.

—Warren Bennis, Author

You will never stub your toe standing still. The faster you go, the more chance there is of stubbing your toe, but the more chance you have of getting somewhere.

—Charles Kettering,
Author

Think of accelerated change as an object hurtling toward you at tremendous speed. If you first spot it a mile away, its speed and the distance between you and it blur its nature; all you can see is an indistinct shape. As the object continues rushing toward you, you begin to discern a rough oblong shape, but you can't determine much else about it. Is it a threatening enemy missile or a friendly vehicle you might ride toward the future? Quickly, it bears down on you. As you peer at it closely, you suddenly see handles

on its side. An opportunity, not a danger! If you
have focused well enough and soon enough,
you can seize it, letting it whisk you forward well
ahead of those who failed to focus on it in time.

—Craig Hickman and
Michael Silva, Authors

We must learn to explore all the options and
possibilities that confront us in a complex and
rapidly changing world. We must learn to welcome
and not fear the voices of dissent.

—J. W. Fulbright, U.S.
Senator, Author

You can change anything you want, but you can't
change everything you want.

—John Rogers, Author

No one learns to make right decisions without being
free to make wrong ones.

—Author Unknown

Sometimes change means doing things different.

—Yogi Berra, Baseball Player

The art of progress is to preserve order amid change and to preserve change amid order.

> —Alfred North Whitehead,
> Bristish Mathematician,
> Philosopher

~~~~~~~~~~~~

Maturity is the ability to live in peace with that which we cannot change. Managing change in complex organizations is like steering a sailboat in turbulent water and stormy winds. If you're on a course to some destination and the wind is blowing at gale force dead broadside; you have to make a number of critical choices. If you head into the wind, you'll lose speed and direction although you probably can ride out the storm. If you let the wind carry you too far, it might blow the boat over; and if you let it go a little less far than that, it may well drive you off course. If you decide to hold rigidly to your course at all costs, you may find that the winds rip the sails and even break off the mast. The true sailor, knowing these choices, works with the wind. He or she will bring the boat up close between gusts, "fall off" a little on the next gust, and come back up to course in such a way that the boat stays on the compass heading towards its destination through many short-term decisions, which go with or against the prevailing winds in an appropriate combination.

> —Richard Beckhard and
> Reuben Harris, Authors

*If you don't have the power to change yourself,
then nothing will change around you.*

> —Anwar Sadat,
> Egyptian President,
> Nobel Peace-Prize Recipient

~~~~~~~~~~

*The person who does not make a choice, makes a
choice.*

> —Jewish Proverb

~~~~~~~~~~

*We must be the change we wish to see in the
world.*

> —Mahatma Gandhi

~~~~~~~~~~

*If my mind can conceive it, and my heart can
believe it, then I can achieve it.*

> —Muhammed Ali, Boxer

~~~~~~~~~~

*Vision without action is merely a dream. Action
without vision just passes the time. Vision with
action can change the world.*

> —Joel Arthur Barker,
> Motivational Speaker,
> Author

Lord grant me the serenity to accept the things I cannot change, the courage to change the things I can, and the wisdom to know the difference.

— *St. Francis of Assisi*

We live in a time of paradox, contradiction, opportunity, and above all, change. To the fearful, change is threatening because they worry that things may get worse. To the hopeful, change is encouraging because they feel things may get better. To those who have confidence in themselves, change is a stimulus because they believe one person can make a difference and influence what goes on around them. These people are the doers and the motivators.

— Author Unknown

Change is the law of life, and those who look only to the past or the present are certain to miss the future.

— John F. Kennedy

Successful change requires: painstakingly laying a foundation; planning in incredible detail; tediously covering and recovering all the bases; continuously explaining and re-explaining; dealing with naysayers; playing politics; soothing egos; dispelling fears; cheerleading; troubleshooting; communicating; compromising; coaxing; cajoling; and ultimately, dragging a few stragglers kicking and screaming into the future. That's hard work. It's also leadership!

— *Robert Ramsey,*
Educator, Author

The curious paradox is that when I accept myself just as I am, then I can change.

> —Carl Rogers,
> Psychologist

~~~~~~~~~~

Deliberation is the work of many men; action, of one alone.

> —General Charles De Gaulle

~~~~~~~~~~

Progress always involves risk; you can't steal second base and keep your foot on first.

> —Frederick Wilcox, Author

~~~~~~~~~~

We must always change, renew, rejuvenate ourselves; otherwise we harden.

> —Goethe

~~~~~~~~~~

Most people are willing to adapt not because they see the light but because they feel the heat.

> —Barbara Johnson,
> Author

It is better to be prepared for an opportunity and not have one than to have an opportunity and not be prepared.

> —Whitney Young Jr.,
> Director, National
> Urban League

The most significant change in a person's life is a change of attitude. Right attitudes produce right actions.

> —Author Unknown

All change involves problems, and all successful change involves solving those problems. If you don't tackle problems, you might have less conflict, but you don't get anywhere in terms of change. That is why risk-taking is important. Those who are successful at implementing change do not have fewer problems. The difference is they have a problem-solving attitude and a problem-solving mechanism.

> —Michael Fullan, Author,
> Professor of Education

The individuals who will succeed and flourish will also be masters of change: adept at reorienting their own and other's activities in untried directions to bring about higher levels of achievement. They will be able to acquire and use power to produce innovation.

—Rosabeth Moss Kanter,
Author, Harvard Professor

You may have habits that weaken you. The secret of change is to focus all your energy, not on fighting the old, but on building the new.

—Socrates

ADVICE FOR LIFE

Advice is like the snow. The softer it falls, the deeper it sinks into the mind.

—Samuel Taylor
Coleridge

Always imitate the behavior of winners when you lose.

—Author Unknown

If you tell the truth, you won't have to remember anything.

—Mark Twain

Finish each day and be done with it. You have done what you could; some blunders and absurdities have crept in; forget them as soon as you can. Tomorrow is a new day; you should begin it serenely and with too high a spirit to be encumbered with your old nonsense.

—Ralph Waldo Emerson

Though no one can go back and make a brand new start, anyone can start from now and make a brand new end.

—Carl Bard, Author

We should be lenient in our judgment, because often the mistakes of others would have been ours had we had the opportunity to make them.

—Dr. Alsaker, Author

Don't major in the minors.

—Mac Mackain,
Educator

—————————

Experience is the name everyone gives to their mistakes.

—Oscar Wilde

—————————

Remember to breathe not weak, snatched gasps, but deep riveting drafts.

—Author Unknown

—————————

The greatest mistake you can make in life is to continually fear you will make one.

—Elbert Hubbard,
Publisher

—————————

Life is what happens to you while you are making other plans.

—John Lennon

—————————

You live longer once you realize that any time spent being unhappy is wasted.

—Ruth E. Renkl, Author

Temper is what gets most of us in trouble. Pride is what keeps us there.

—Mark Twain

Rely on the message of the teacher, not on his personality. Rely on the meaning, not just on the words. Rely on the real meaning, not on the provisional one. Rely on your wisdom mind, not on your ordinary, judgmental mind.

—Buddha

Do what you can with what you have where you are.

—Theodore Roosevelt

When you work with people it is a lot like mining for gold . . . when you mine for gold, you must literally move tons of dirt to find a single ounce of gold. However, you do not look for the dirt—you look for the gold!

—Andrew Carnegie,
Industrialist, Philanthropist

Out of clutter, find simplicity. From discord, find harmony. In the middle of difficulty lies opportunity.

—Albert Einstein

Compliment what cannot be photographed.

—Connie Dembrowsky,
Educator, Author

━━━━━━━━━━

Learn to pause . . . or nothing worthwhile will catch up to you.

—Doug King, Poet

━━━━━━━━━━

If you want happiness . . .
For an hour . . . take a nap
For a day . . . go fishing
For a month . . . get married
For a year . . . inherit a fortune
For a lifetime . . . help someone else.
When faced with a decision—decide.
When faced with a choice—choose.
Sitting on the fence
Will leave you too tense
Because you neither win nor lose.

—Barry Spilchuk,
Author, Motivational Speaker

━━━━━━━━━━

Since we have two ears and one mouth, we should listen twice as much as we talk.

—Author Unknown

It is better to light a candle than curse the darkness.

> —Eleanor Roosevelt

Don't be a drip—go with the flow.

> —John Blaydes,
> Educator, Author,
> Motivational Speaker

Don't be troubled if the temptation to give advice is irresistible; the ability to ignore it is universal.

> —Author Unknown

Changing schools is like moving a cemetery.

> —Author Unknown

To profit from good advice requires more wisdom than to give it.

> —John Churton Collins,
> Lecturer, Critic

Advice should always be consumed between two thick slices of doubt.

> —Walt Schmidt, Author

If you want truly to understand something, try to change it.

> —Kurt Lewin,
> Social Psychologist

———————

Bringing about systemic change in schools is like fixing a bicycle while you're riding it.

> —Robert Ramsey,
> Educator, Author

———————

Advice is what we ask for when we already know the answer but wish we didn't.

> —Erica Jong, Author

———————

Each time a person stands up for an ideal, or acts to improve the lot of others, or strikes out against injustice, he/she sends forth a tiny ripple of hope. . . . and crossing each other from a million different centers of energy and daring, those ripples build a current that can sweep down the mightiest walls of oppression and resistance.

> —Robert Kennedy

———————

We give advice by the bucket but take it by the grain.

> —William Alger, Minister

It's a pleasure to give advice, humiliating to need it, normal to ignore it.

—Author Unknown

⋅⋅⋅⋅⋅⋅⋅⋅⋅⋅

Go out on a limb. That's where the fruit is.

—Jimmy Townsend,
Author

⋅⋅⋅⋅⋅⋅⋅⋅⋅⋅

You have to accept whatever comes and the only important thing is that you meet it with courage and with the best you have to give.

—Eleanor Roosevelt

⋅⋅⋅⋅⋅⋅⋅⋅⋅⋅

To do good things is noble. To advise others to do good is even nobler—and a lot easier.

—Mark Twain

⋅⋅⋅⋅⋅⋅⋅⋅⋅⋅

The sure way to miss success is to miss the opportunity.

—Author Unknown

⋅⋅⋅⋅⋅⋅⋅⋅⋅⋅

Love is the most important ingredient of success. Without it your life echoes emptiness. With it, your life vibrates warmth and meaning. Even in hardship, love shines through. Therefore, search for love.

Because if you don't have it, you're not really living—you're only breathing.

—*Wynn Davis, Author*

It is easier to beg for forgiveness than to ask permission.

—*Jesuit Saying*

The best time not to do drugs or alcohol is the first time.

—*Mickey Mantle,*
Baseball Player

When you get to the end of your rope, tie a knot and hang on.

—*Franklin D. Roosevelt*

There is nothing either good or bad but thinking makes it so.

—*William Shakespeare*

The trouble with advice is that you can't tell if it's good or bad until you've taken it.

—*Frank Tyger, Author*

In three words I can sum up everything I've learned about life: It goes on.

—Robert Frost

Get someone else to blow your horn and the sound will carry twice as far.

—Will Rogers, Comedian

Life is like the baseball season, where even the best team loses at least a third of its games, and even the worst team has its days of brilliance. The goal is not to win every game but to win more than you lose, and if you do that often enough, in the end you may find you have won it all.

—Rabbi Harold Kushner

Accept the pain, cherish the joys, resolve the regrets; then can come the best of benedictions—If I had my life to live over, I'd do it all the same.

—John McIntosh, Author

If your outgo exceeds your income, then your upkeep will be your downfall.

—World War II Poster

As you simplify your life, the laws of the universe will be simpler.

—Henry David Thoreau

———————————————

There's only a slight difference between keeping your chin up and sticking your neck out, but it's a difference worth knowing.

—Author Unknown

———————————————

Be like a postage stamp. Stick to something until you get there.

—John Noe, Author

———————————————

Those who hate you don't win unless you hate them—and then you destroy yourself.

—Richard Nixon

———————————————

Most of us ask for advice when we know the answer but want a different one.

—Ivern Bell, Author

———————————————

Accept good advice gracefully—as long as it doesn't interfere with what you intended to do in the first place.

—Gene Brown, Author

Most people ask for happiness on condition.
Happiness can be felt only if you don't set conditions.

—Arthur Rubinstein,
Pianist

Don't fear failure so much that you refuse to try new
things. The saddest summary of a life contains three
descriptions: could have, might have, and should have.

—Louis E. Boone,
Educator, Author

Go confidently in the direction of your dreams! Live
the life you imagined.

—Henry David Thoreau

He that gives good advice, builds with one hand;
he that gives good counsel and example, builds
with both.

—Francis Bacon

When in the world are we going to begin to live as if
we understood that this is life? This is our time, our
day, and it is passing. What are we waiting for?

—Author Unknown

Don't lower your expectations to meet your
performance. Raise your level of performance

to meet your expectations. Expect the best of
yourself, and then do what is necessary to make
it a reality.

—Ralph Marston, Author

~~~~~~~~~~

Life is a great big canvas, and you should throw all
the paint on it you can.

—Danny Kaye, Actor,
Comedian

~~~~~~~~~~

Life is not a destination, it's a journey. It's not a
series of goals, it's a series of steps, of events
unfolding as you make your way.

—Author Unknown

~~~~~~~~~~

If I had six hours to chop down a tree, I'd spend
the first four sharpening the axe.

—Abraham Lincoln

~~~~~~~~~~

The purpose of life is not to be happy. The purpose
of life is to matter, to be productive, to have it
make a difference that you lived at all.

—Author Unknown

~~~~~~~~~~

Happiness means self-fulfillment and is given to
those who use to the fullest whatever talents God
or luck or fate bestows upon them.

—Leo Rosten, Author

7
PRINCIPLES FOR PRINCIPALS

Celebrate your success and find
humor in your failures. Don't
take yourself so seriously.
Loosen up and everyone around
you will loosen up. Have fun and
always show enthusiasm. When
all else fails, put on a costume
and sing a silly song.

—*Sam Walton,*
Businessman (Wal Mart)

Your life is your message. Leadership by example is not only the most pervasive but also the most enduring form of leadership.

—Mahatma Gandhi

———————

Our very survival as principals may hinge on our ability to understand and deal with change.

—Author Unknown

———————

Don't be afraid to take a big step. You can't cross a chasm in two small jumps.

—David Lloyd George,
Former British Prime
Minister

———————

There is little difference in people, but that little difference makes a big difference. That little difference is attitude. The big difference is whether it is positive or negative.

—Mark Twain

———————

The greater thing in this world is not so much where we stand as in what direction we are going.

—Oliver Wendell Holmes

Leaders know that while their position gives them authority, their behavior earns them respect. It is consistency between words and actions that builds a leader's credibility.

—James Kouzes and
Barry Posner, Authors

Man cannot discover new oceans, unless he has the courage to lose sight of the shore.

—Andre Gide,
Nobel Prize-Winning Author

Make a careful list of all things done to you that you abhorred. Don't do them to others, ever. Make another list of things done for you that you loved. Do them for others, always.

—Dee Hock, Author

A vision without a task is a dream. A task without a vision is drudgery. But a task with vision can change the world.

—Black Elk

When you encounter difficulties and contradictions, don't try to break them, rather bend them with gentleness and time.

—Bishop St. Francis de Sales

It is not what name others call you that matters, but what name you respond to that truly determines who you are.

—*Swahili Saying*

If we could sell our experiences for what they cost us, we'd all be millionaires.

—*Abigail Van Buren,*
Newspaper Columnist

Things turn out best for the people who make the best out of the way things turn out!

—*John Wooden,*
Basketball Coach

Our greatest weakness lies in giving up. The most certain way to succeed is always to try just one more time.

—*Thomas Edison*

Anything we can conceive, we can achieve.

—*Napoleon Hill, Author,*
Motivational Speaker

An eye for an eye makes the whole world blind.

—*Mahatma Gandhi*

For every minute that you are angry, you lose sixty seconds of happiness.

—Ralph Waldo Emerson

In the midst of great joy, do not promise anyone anything. In the midst of great anger, do not answer anyone's letter.

—Chinese Proverb

Let me spread happiness where I go, not when.

—Author Unknown

You are today where your thoughts have brought you; you will be tomorrow where your thoughts take you.

—James Allen, Essayist

Would that there were an award for people who come to understand the concept of enough. Good enough. Successful enough. Thin enough. Rich enough. Socially responsible enough. When you have self-respect, you have enough.

—Gail Sheehy, Author

The secret of managing is to keep the guys who hate you away from the guys who are undecided.

—Casey Stengal,
Baseball Coach

I don't know the key to success, but the key to failure is trying to please everybody.

—Bill Cosby, Comedian

~~~~~~~~~~~~

The greatest good we can do for others is not to share our riches with them, but to reveal theirs to them.

—Zig Ziglar,
Motivational Speaker, Author

~~~~~~~~~~~~

The way we live our days is the way we live our lives.

—Annie Dillard,
Writer, Poet

~~~~~~~~~~~~

We grew up in a world of stability with spasms of change. Today we live in a world of change with spasms of stability.

—Author Unknown

~~~~~~~~~~~~

Sometimes when you think about all the bad things that you read in the newspaper and then you walk inside a classroom and see this you realize that there are so many good things in the world.

—Grandpa Leo,
Kindergarten Classroom Volunteer

I am sure that if people had to choose between living where the noise of children never stopped and where it was never heard, all the good-natured and sound people would prefer incessant noise to incessant silence.

—George Bernard Shaw

―――――――――

School need not be merely a place where big people who are learned teach little people who are learners.

—Roland Barth, Author

―――――――――

I can live for two months on a good compliment.

—Mark Twain

―――――――――

Few, if any, of us ever realize the far-reaching effects of our existence. The consequences of our choices and actions spread out into the world like ripples of water, affecting many people in ways we could never imagine. Your influence is etched in the lives of those who have been fortunate to be your pupil, your colleague, and your friend.

—Author Unknown

―――――――――

Never discourage anyone who continually makes progress, no matter how slow.

—Plato

We are fortunate to work in a noble and honorable profession where we have the power, the ability, and the compassion necessary to make the world a better place.

> —John Blaydes,
> Educator, Author,
> Motivational Speaker

The illiterate of the future will not be those who cannot read and write, but those who cannot learn, unlearn, and relearn.

> —Alvin Toffler,
> Author, Futurist

Tell me, and I'll forget. Show me, and I may not remember. Involve me, and I'll understand.

> —Native American Saying

Alone we can do so little; together we can do so much.

> —Helen Keller

Thinking is the hardest work there is, which is the probable reason why so few engage in it.

> —Henry Ford

An excellent rule to follow is, if you can't write it and sign it, don't say it!

> —Earl Wilson,
> Newspaper Columnist

A man has to live with himself, and he should see to it that he always has good company.

> —Charles Evans,
> Former U.S. Supreme
> Court Chief Justice

Always do right. That will gratify some people and astonish the rest.

> —Mark Twain

We're drowning in information and starving for knowledge.

> —Rutherford D. Rogers,
> Yale University
> Librarian

Education is simply the soul of a society as it passes from one generation to another.

> —G. K. Chesterton,
> Author

As school principals, the focus of our job should be to enable teachers to teach and students to learn.

—John Blaydes,
Educator, Author,
Motivational Speaker

Perseverance is the hard work you do after you get tired of doing the hard work you already did.

—Newt Gingrich,
Former Speaker of the House
of Representatives

You cannot do a kindness too soon, for you never know how soon it will be too late.

—Ralph Waldo Emerson

The trouble with most of us is that we would rather be ruined by praise than saved by criticism.

—Dr. Norman Vincent Peale,
Author, Minister

Today's pressures on the principalship show no signs of decreasing their intensity. Future challenges include encouraging dispersed yet centered leadership, creating a cohesive community out of increasingly diverse populations, being responsible without being in charge, changing rapidly in response to social needs without leaving people behind, building trust and confidence in an openly cynical society, and caring for people while challenging them to grow. Together, these challenges will continue to fill every principal's day with problems to solve, puzzles to unravel, and paradoxes to manage and endure.

—Terrence Deal
and Kent Peterson, Authors

Wise are those who learn that the bottom line doesn't always have to be their top priority.

—William Arthur Ward,
Author

After all is said and done, more is said than done.

—Author Unknown

Listen long enough and the person will generally come up with an adequate solution.

—Mary Kay Ash,
Businesswoman
(Mary Kay Cosmetics)

A messy desk is a sign of a messy desk—no more, no less. It is not a reflection on your intellect, talent, or ancestry.

—Dr. Dru Scott, Author

FOR A GOOD LAUGH

I think that I have found inner peace. My therapist told me a way to achieve inner peace was to finish things that I had started. Today I finished 2 bags of potato chips, a lemon pie, a fifth of Jack Daniels, and a small box of chocolate candy. I feel better already.

—*Author Unknown*

Laughter causes the lungs to pump out carbon dioxide, the eyes to cleanse themselves with tears, the muscles to relax, the flow of adrenaline to increase, and the cardiovascular system to be exercised. Perhaps most important for those in schools, endorphins, the chemicals produced by the brain to relieve pain, are released into the bloodstream when a person laughs. Clearly, laughter is good for schools and for those who inhabit them.

—Roland Barth, Author

Laughter is an instant vacation.

—Milton Berle, Comedian

We don't stop laughing because we grow old; we grow old because we stop laughing.

—Michael Pritchard,
Keynote Speaker

The 5 most common words heard by a school principal: "Have you got a minute?"

—Author Unknown

Accept that some days you're the pigeon and some days you're the statue.

—Author Unknown

A conclusion is the place where you got tired of thinking.

> —Arthur Block, Author

———————————————

A smile is a curve that sets everything straight.

> —Phyllis Diller,
> Comedienne

———————————————

A smile is a light on your face to let someone know that you are home.

> —Author Unknown

———————————————

The future ain't what it used to be.

> —Yogi Berra,
> Baseball Player

———————————————

Thrift is a wonderful virtue, especially in one's ancestors.

> —Author Unknown

———————————————

People who are resting on their laurels are wearing them on the wrong end.

> —Malcolm Kushner,
> Humorist

Experience is something you don't get until just after you need it.

—Author Unknown

Outside of a dog, a man's best friend is a book. Inside of a dog, it's too dark to read.

—Groucho Marx,
Comedian

Wise men talk because they have something to say; fools talk because they have to say something.

—Plato

There are two different kinds of people in this world: those who finish what they start, and. . . .

—Author Unknown

If ignorance is bliss, why aren't more people happy?

—Author Unknown

If you don't think every day is a great day, try going without one.

—Jim Evans, Author

Seven days without laughter makes one weak.

—Joel Goodman,
Humorist

If you laugh a lot, when you get older your wrinkles will be in the right places.

—Andrew Mason, Author

Have you ever noticed that anybody going slower than you is an idiot, and anyone going faster than you is a maniac?

—George Carlin,
Comedian

Every morning I get up and look through the Forbes list of the richest people in America. If I'm not there, I go to work.

—Robert Orben, Author

Worrying is like a rocking chair—it gives you something to do, but it gets you nowhere.

—Glenn Turner, Author

A smile confuses an approaching frown.

—Author Unknown

Mirth can be a major tool for insight, changing "ha ha" to "aha."

—Joel Goodman,
Humorist

To steal ideas from one person is plagiarism; to steal from many is research.

—Author Unknown

The severity of the itch is inversely proportional to the ability to reach it.

—Author Unknown

Any child who is anxious to mow the lawn is too young to do it.

—Bob Phillips,
Author, Humorist

There are 3 kinds of people: those who can count and those who can't.

—Author Unknown

When I hear somebody sigh, "Life is hard," I am always tempted to ask, "Compared to what?"

—Sydney Harris,
Journalist

He always has too much month left at the end of his money.

—Author Unknown

~~~~~~~~~~~~~

A pat on the back is only a few centimeters from a kick in the butt.

—Dilbert,
Cartoon Character

~~~~~~~~~~~~~

Bumper sticker on teacher's car: We upped our test scores—up yours.

—Author Unknown

~~~~~~~~~~~~~

He who laughs last probably didn't get the joke.

—Author Unknown

~~~~~~~~~~~~~

A committee is a group of the unfit, appointed by the unwilling, to do the unnecessary.

—Steve Harrol, Author

~~~~~~~~~~~~~

It is good sportsmanship to not pick up lost golf balls while they are still rolling.

—Mark Twain

Don't sweat petty things . . . or pet sweaty things.

> —*Author Unknown*

~~~~~~~~~~~~

If it wasn't for the last minute, nothing would get done.

> —*Dilbert,*
> *Cartoon Character*

~~~~~~~~~~~~

To get something done, a committee should consist of no more than three persons, two of whom are absent.

> —*Robert Copeland,*
> *Author*

~~~~~~~~~~~~

If the members of some committees were laid end to end, it would help.

> —*Author Unknown*

~~~~~~~~~~~~

Given the opportunity to embarrass you publicly, technology will invariably do so—usually in direct proportion to the importance of the presentation or the audience.

> —*Michael Hoy, Author*

Even if you are on the right track, you'll get run over if you just sit there.

—Will Rogers, Comedian

———————

Knowledge has never been known to enter the head through an open mouth.

—Doug Larsen, Author

———————

Sometimes it is better to remain quiet and look like a fool, than to open one's mouth and remove all doubt.

—Mark Twain

———————

Someday is not a day of the week.

—Author Unknown

———————

Stressed is desserts spelled backwards.

—Author Unknown

———————

We don't lose our sense of humor when we get older—we get older when we lose our sense of humor.

—Author Unknown

It's great to be great, but it's greater to be human.

—Will Rogers, Comedian

I always wanted to be somebody—I guess I should have been more specific.

—Lily Tomlin,
Actress, Comedienne

Dear God, I want to pray for patience and I want it right now!

—Oren Arnold, Author

Your brain starts working the day you're born and stops working the moment you stand up to speak.

—George Jessel,
Comedian, Toastmaster

The only difference between a rut and a grave is the depth of the hole.

—Roland Barth, Author

The School Leader's Mantra: Do not walk behind me for I may not lead. Do not walk ahead of me for I may not follow. Do not walk beside me either. Just leave me alone. I need my space.

—Author Unknown

Laughter is the sun that drives winter from the human face.

—Victor Hugo

~~~~~~~~~~

Humor is a reminder that no matter how high the throne one sits on, one sits on one's bottom.

—Taki, Author

~~~~~~~~~~

I took a speed-reading course and read War and Peace in twenty minutes. It's about Russia.

—Woody Allen,
Comedian,
Film Director

~~~~~~~~~~

In the first place God made idiots. This was for practice. Then he made school boards.

—Mark Twain

~~~~~~~~~~

Laughter is the shortest distance between two people.

—Victor Borge,
Pianist, Comedian

~~~~~~~~~~

A filing cabinet is a repository where papers are lost alphabetically.

—Author Unknown

Laughter is a tranquilizer with no side effects.

—Arnold Glasow, Author

❈❈❈❈❈❈❈❈❈

Before you criticize someone, you should walk a mile in their shoes. That way, when you do criticize them, you are a mile away and you have their shoes.

—Author Unknown

❈❈❈❈❈❈❈❈❈

The person who knows how to laugh at himself. He will never cease to be amused.

—Shirley Maclaine,
Actress, Author

❈❈❈❈❈❈❈❈❈

When you narrow it down, there are only three kinds of leaders in schools today: those who make things happen, those who watch things happen, and those who wonder what happened.

—Author Unknown

❈❈❈❈❈❈❈❈❈

Any child can tell you that the sole purpose of a middle name is so he can tell when he's really in trouble.

—Dennis Fakes, Author

It has been observed that he who laughs, lasts.

—Author Unknown

I couldn't be two-faced. If I had two faces, I wouldn't wear this one.

—Abraham Lincoln

Imagination was given to man to compensate for what he is not. A sense of humor was provided to console him for what he is.

—Horace Walpole,
English Writer

A good sense of humor helps to overlook the unbecoming, understand the unconventional, tolerate the unpleasant, overcome the unexpected, and outlast the unbearable.

—Billy Graham,
Evangelist

It has always seemed to me that hearty laughter is a good way to jog internally without having to go outdoors.

—Norman Cousins,
Author

Everybody is ignorant, only on different subjects.

—Will Rogers, Humorist

———————

I like long walks, especially when they are taken by people who annoy me.

—Fred Allen, Comedian

———————

He was such a very conscious lad,
He never romped or played.
He never smoked, he never drank,
He never kissed the maid.
So when he upped and passed away,
his insurance was denied.
They claimed because he never really lived,
he never really died.

—Robert Cavett,
Author, Founder,
National Speakers Bureau

———————

Schools ain't what they used to be—but they never were.

—Mark Twain

———————

I have a simple philosophy. Fill what's empty. Empty what's full. And scratch where it itches.

—Alice Roosevelt Longworth,
Socialite, Theodore Roosevelt's Daughter

What the world needs is more geniuses with humility. There are so few of us left.

—Oscar Levant,
Pianist, Comedian

It is better to wear out than to rust out.

—Bishop Richard Cumberland

We are all worms, but I do believe I am a glow worm.

—Winston Churchill

Don't accept your dog's admiration as conclusive evidence that you are wonderful.

—Ann Landers,
Newspaper Columnist

Laughter is part of the human survival kit.

—Author Unknown

An optimist goes to the window every morning and says, "Good morning, God." The pessimist goes to the window every morning and says, "Good God! Morning!"

—Author Unknown

I have always felt that laughter in the face of reality is probably the finest sound there is and will last until the day when the game is called on account of darkness. In this world, a good time to laugh is any time you can.

—Linda Ellerbee,
　　Journalist, Author,
　　Speaker

If A equals success, then the formula is A = X + Y + Z. X is work. Y is play. Z is keep your mouth shut.

—Albert Einstein

If you wish to glimpse inside a human soul and get to know a man, don't bother analyzing his ways of being silent, of talking, of weeping, or seeing how much he is moved by noble ideas; you'll get better results if you just watch him laugh. If he laughs well, he's a good man.

—Fyodor Dostoyevsky

Change is inevitable—except from a vending machine.

—Arnold Beckman,
　　Scientist, Philanthropist

The purpose of a meeting is to assemble people who aren't doing anything, to talk about doing something, and hence feel that they have accomplished something. It aims to accomplish by talk what has not been accomplished by action.

—Author Unknown

When you use your sense of humor, be sure that you use your sense as well as your humor.

—Author Unknown

Some students drink at the fountain of knowledge while others just gargle.

—Arthur Unknown

The higher you climb the flagpole, the more people see your rear end.

—Don Meredith, Author

Parents were invented to make children happy by giving them something to ignore.

—Ogden Nash, Poet

I was halfway through life before I discovered that it is a do-it-yourself job.

—Author Unknown

If you don't know where you are, you might not be there.

> —*Yogi Berra,*
> *Baseball Player*

~~~~~~~~~~~~~~~~~~~~

To get 'em listening, get 'em laughing.

> —*Allen Klein,*
> *Motivational Speaker,*
> *Author*

~~~~~~~~~~~~~~~~~~~~

It's amazing what you can observe just by watching.

> —*Yogi Berra,*
> *Baseball Player*

~~~~~~~~~~~~~~~~~~~~

I wake up every morning determined both to change the world and have one hell of a good time. Sometimes this makes planning the day a little difficult.

> —*E. B. White, Author*

INSPIRATIONAL
LEADERSHIP

Leadership is doing all you can to have the heart of a lion, the skin of a rhino, and the soul of an angel.

—*Robert Cooper, Author*

It's the action, not the fruit of the action that's important. You have to do the right thing. It may not be in your power, may not be in your time, that there'll be any fruit. But that doesn't mean you stop doing the right thing. You may never know what results come from your action. But if you do nothing, there will be no result.

—Mahatma Gandhi

In any moment of decision, the best thing you can do is the right thing, the next best thing is the wrong thing, and the worst thing you can do is nothing.

—Theodore Roosevelt

Our chief want is someone who will inspire us to be what we know we can be.

—Ralph Waldo Emerson

Leadership is the art of getting someone else to do something that you want done because they want to do it.

—Dwight D. Eisenhower

Things which matter most must never be at the mercy of things which matter least.

—Goethe

*What you do speaks so loudly, they can't hear
what you say.*

—Ralph Waldo Emerson

---

*A leader is someone who has the capacity to
create a compelling vision that takes people to a
new place, and to translate that vision into
action. Leaders draw other people to them by
enrolling them in their vision. What leaders do is
inspire people, empower them. They pull rather
than push.*

—Warren Bennis, Author

---

*The basic role of the leader is to foster mutual
respect and build a complementary team where each
strength is made productive and each weakness
made irrelevant.*

—Stephen Covey,
Author, Motivational Speaker

---

*The greatest danger for most of us is not that our
aim is too high and we will miss it, but that it is too
low and we will reach it.*

—Michelangelo

Example is a powerful teacher! If as inspirational leaders we are dedicated to helping others grow through their work, then we must strive to model the values, attitudes and actions that we wish to see in those we lead. Let both sides explore what problems unite us instead of belaboring those problems which divide us.

—John F. Kennedy

There was, they argue, a time when our schools were better. Nonsense! There are more good schools today than at any time in the past. If there are also more bad schools it is because there are more schools trying to educate children who, in the good old days, would have been working in factories and sweatshops.

—Phil Schlecty,
        Motivational Speaker,
        Author

Empowering leaders bring joy, enthusiasm, and optimism to the world of those they touch, every day. Empowering leaders are proactive, inspiring, and willing to take the initiative. Empowering leaders have the ability to both give and get authority and the responsibility necessary to improve performance on every level.

—Larry W. Dennis,
        Author

Words and plans are not enough. Leaders stand up for their beliefs. They practice what they preach. They show others by their own example that they live by the values that they profess.

> —James Kouzes and
> Barry Posner, Authors

―――――――――

The power of personal example is the essence of true leadership.

> —Stephen Covey,
> Author, Motivational
> Speaker

―――――――――

Education is knowing what to do when you don't have the answer.

> —Art Costa,
> Author, Educator

―――――――――

Coming together is a beginning. Staying together is a process. Working together is success.

> —Henry Ford

Success on any major scale requires you to accept responsibility. . . . In the final analysis, the one quality that all successful people have . . . is the ability to take on responsibility.

—Michael Korda, Author

------~~~~~~~------

Managers are people who do things right and leaders are people who do the right thing.

—Warren Bennis and
Joan Goldsmith,
Authors

------~~~~~~~------

The "impossible" dream can only be attained in "possible" stages.

—Author Unknown

------~~~~~~~------

No man will make a great leader who wants to do it all himself or to get all the credit for doing it.

—Andrew Carnegie,
Industrialist,
Philanthropist

------~~~~~~~------

If a leader has a special gift, it is the ability to sense the purpose in others. So truly inspirational leadership is not really selling people some science fiction future. Rather, it is showing people how the vision can directly benefit them, how their specific needs can be satisfied. It is like holding up a mirror and reflecting back to them what they said that they most desire. When they see the reflection, they recognize it and are immediately attracted to it.

—James Kouzes and
Barry Posner, Authors

Leaders have a significant role in creating the state of mind that is the school. They can serve as symbols of the moral unity of the school. They can express the values that hold the school together. Most important, they can conceive and articulate goals that lift people out of their petty preoccupations, carry them out of the conflicts that tear a school apart, and unite them in pursuit of objectives worthy of their best efforts.

—John W. Gardner,
Author, Founder,
Common Cause

To know what to do is wisdom. To know how to do it is skill. To know when to do it is judgment. To strive to do it best is dedication. To do it for the benefit of others is compassion. To do it quietly is humility. To get the job done is achievement. To get others to do all of the above is leadership.

—Author Unknown

*Man's mind stretched to a new idea never goes
back to its original dimensions.*

—Oliver Wendell Holmes,
Author, Poet

———————————

*Buried deep within each of us is a spark of
greatness, a spark that can be fanned into flames of
passion and achievement. The spark is not outside
of you, it is born deep within you.*

—James A Ray,
Motivational Speaker

———————————

*If you treat an individual as he is, he will stay as he
is, but if you treat him as if he were what he ought
to be and could be, he will become what he ought
to be and what he could be.*

—Goethe

———————————

*I have a dream that one day this nation will rise up
and live out the true meaning of this creed—We
hold these truths to be self-evident: that all men are
created equal.*

—Martin Luther King Jr.

———————————

*I believe that the act of leadership is, in part, an
effort to impose order on chaos, to provide direction
to what otherwise appears to be adrift, and to give*

*meaning and coherence to events that otherwise
appear, and may in fact be, random.*

—Phil Schlecty, Author

———————————————

*Effective leaders create power . . . and give it away.
Leadership can be defined as providing people with
a picture of what needs to be done to achieve
common objectives and instilling the desire to
achieve them chiefly by actions rather than rhetoric.
Most effective actions occur after clear visualization
is provided of the results expected to occur from
those actions.*

—Kenneth Robertson,
Author

———————————————

*Sixty years ago I knew everything; now I know
nothing. Education is a progressive discovery of our
own ignorance.*

—Will Durant,
Author, Historian

———————————————

*Your success as a leader who gets the most from
people won't depend upon your title, your
degrees, or your previous experience. It won't be
the result of how much you know, how hard you
work, what long hours you keep, or anything you
say. It will rest almost totally on the way you
treat people.*

—Robert Ramsey,
Educator, Author

Real leaders are ordinary people with extraordinary determination.

> —Author Unknown

~~~~~~~~~~

What the mind attends, the mind considers. What the mind does not consider, the mind dismisses. What the mind continues to consider, the mind believes. What the mind believes, the mind eventually does.

> —Earl Nightingale,
> Author, Motivational
> Speaker

~~~~~~~~~~

A leader has been defined as one who knows the way, goes the way, and shows the way.

> —Author Unknown

~~~~~~~~~~

One's philosophy is not best expressed in words. It is expressed in the choices one makes. The process never ends until we die. And the choices we make are ultimately our responsibility.

> —Eleanor Roosevelt

~~~~~~~~~~

Each step on the path to a higher standard of leadership takes courage—courage to commit to absolute values and to the universal code of conduct to treat others as ourselves. Your courage will serve as a source of inspiration to others and

*will help those you associate with to achieve a
higher standard as well.*

                    —Keshavan Nair, Author

—————~~~~~~~—————

*The single most important person in any school is the
principal. You're the instructional leader, you're the
coach in the sense that you have a team that you
have to bring to its fullest potential. You have to be a
politician and I'm sorry for that, but you do.*

                    —Senator Hillary Clinton

—————~~~~~~~—————

*Words and plans are not enough. Leaders stand up
for their beliefs. They practice what they preach. They
show others by their own example that they live by
the values that they profess. Leaders know that while
their position gives them authority, their behavior
earns them respect. It is consistency between words
and actions that builds a leader's credibility.*

                    —James Kouzes and
                    Barry Posner, Authors

—————~~~~~~~—————

*Don't keep forever on the public road, going only
where others have gone. Leave the beaten track
occasionally and drive into the woods. You will be
certain to find something you have never seen before.
Of course it will be a little thing, but do not ignore it.
Follow it up, explore all around it; one discovery will
lead to another, and before you know it you will have
something worth thinking about to occupy your mind.
All really big discoveries are the results of thought.*

                    —Alexander Graham Bell

A leader needs a philosophy, a high set of standards by which the organization is measured, a set of values about how employees, colleagues, and customers ought to be treated, a set of principles that make the organization unique and distinctive. Leaders also need plans. They need maps to guide people. Yet complex plans overwhelm people; they stifle action. Instead, leaders lay down milestones and put up signposts. They unravel bureaucratic knots. They create opportunities for small wins, which add up to major victories.

—James Kouzes and
Barry Posner, Authors

There is nothing more difficult to take in hand, more perilous to conduct, or more uncertain in its success than to take the lead in the introduction of a new order of things.

—Machiavelli

The very essence of leadership is that you have a vision. You can't blow an uncertain trumpet.

—Father Theodore Hesburgh,
Civil Rights Activist

Education is about discovering the special skills and talents of students and guiding their learning according to high standards. Education is also about teaching our children and young people basic American values and uncorking that world-renowned American ingenuity that has characterized our country. For America to move forward and continue as a world leader, and for all our communities to become prosperous and strong, more individuals need to become involved in improving our schools and colleges.

> —Richard Riley,
> Former U.S. Secretary
> of Education

We need to take time for self care, reflection, and affirmation. We have a choice. We can allow the stress of the job to crush our ability to be the kind of inspirational leaders we want to be, or we can energetically and enthusiastically demonstrate that we are the positive climate creators at our school. Our challenge is that every day we need to rekindle the passion and get in touch with the joy in our job. Joy is an essential ingredient of inspirational leadership.

> —John Blaydes,
> Educator, Author,
> Motivational Speaker

Leadership is being visible when things are going awry and invisible when they are working well.

> —Tom Peters,
> Author, Motivational
> Speaker

Leadership is a people process. It calls for the application of knowledge, skills, and attitudes that allow each of us to successfully influence and inspire others towards doing the right things. Leadership deals with effectiveness. On the other hand, management is a coordinating process we carry out to make sure the work functions and tasks get done well and in a timely way.

—Millard MacAdam,
Educator, Author

If we are going to seize the promise of our times and educate our children so they can keep their dreams alive, we must all work together. Not government alone, not individuals alone, but as parents and children, as employers and employees, teachers and students, community leaders and community members, as government and citizens. We must renew our schools so every American child has the opportunity to get the best possible education for the twenty-first century.

—Bill Clinton

The significant problems we face cannot be solved by the same level of thinking that created them.

—Albert Einstein

The greatness of Albert Schweitzer—indeed, the essence of Schwietzer—is the man as a symbol. It is not so much what he has done for others, but what others have done because of him and the power of his example. This is the measure of the man. What has come out of his life and thought is the kind of inspiration that can animate a generation. He has supplied a working demonstration of reverence for life.

—Norman Cousins,
Author

It's easy to make a buck. It's a lot tougher to make a difference.

—Tom Brokaw,
Broadcast Journalist

We are in a giving profession—but we can't give what we don't have. It's impossible to be an inspirational leader on an empty spirit. We sometimes forget the importance of living balanced lives when the workload seems all-consuming of our time and energies. We seek to make order out of chaos. We need to take the time for infilling and reflection so that we have the inner resources that will enable us to continue to give to others.

—John Blaydes,
Educator, Author,
Motivational Speaker

We know what a person thinks not when he tells us what he thinks, but by his actions.

—Isaac Bashevis Singer,
Nobel Prize-Winning Author

Learning is the essential fuel for the leader, the source of high-octane energy that keeps up the momentum by continually sparking new understanding, new ideas and new challenges. It is absolutely indispensable under today's conditions of rapid change and complexity. Very simply, those who do not learn do not survive as leaders.

—Warren Bennis, Author

A leader is a person you would follow to a place you wouldn't go by yourself.

—Joel Barker, Author,
Motivational Speaker

The truth of the matter is that you always know the right thing to do. The hard part is doing it.

—General Norman Schwarzkopf

Whatever natural endowments we bring to the role of leadership, they can be enhanced; nurture is far more important than nature in determining who becomes a successful leader.

—Warren Bennis, Author

It often requires more courage to dare to do right than to fear to do wrong.

—Abraham Lincoln

Failure is the opportunity to begin again more intelligently.

—Henry Ford

———————————

The only limit to our realization of tomorrow will be our doubts of today.

—Franklin D. Roosevelt

———————————

What lies behind us and what lies before us are tiny matters compared to what lies within us.

—Ralph Waldo Emerson

———————————

Outstanding leaders go out of the way to boost the self-esteem of their personnel. If people believe in themselves, it's amazing what they can accomplish.

—Sam Walton,
Businessman (Wal Mart)

———————————

The compassionate leader must take action. Compassion implies that you do not walk by on the road of life. When you see a wrong, you try to right it. When you see an injustice, you try to make it just. When you see a child or teenager struggling just to survive each day, you try to help them.

—Dale J. Metz,
Motivational Speaker

Fear of failure brings fear of taking risks and you're never going to get what you want out of life without taking some risks.

> —Lee Iaccoca, Author,
> Businessman

———————

The difference between the impossible and the possible lies in a man's determination.

> —Tommy Lasorda,
> Baseball Coach

———————

Mission is an image of a desired state of affairs that inspires action, determines behavior and fuels motivation.

> —Charles Garfield,
> Author, Founder, Peak
> Experience

———————

It's extremely difficult to lead farther than you have gone yourself.

> —Author Unknown

———————

Diplomacy is the art of taking sides without anyone knowing it.

> —Author Unknown

———————

The key to all motivation is desire, and the master key to creating desire is responsiveness to the needs, desires and interests of the people you would lead.

—John R. Noe, Author

It is time for us all to stand and cheer the doer, the achiever—the one who recognizes the challenge and does something about it.

—Vince Lombardi,
Football Coach

To get others to do what you want them to do, you must see things through their eyes.

—David Schwartz,
Motivational Speaker

When the best leader's work is done the people say, "We did it ourselves."

—Lao-Tzu

Ability is the art of getting credit for all the homeruns somebody else hits.

—Casey Stengel,
Baseball Coach

One's action ought to come out of an achieved stillness, not to be a mere rushing on.

—D. H. Lawrence

The price of greatness is responsibility.

>—Winston Churchill

~~~~~~~~~~~~~

Leadership is the quality that transforms good intentions into positive action; it turns a group of individuals into a team.

>—T. Boone Pickens,
>Author, Businessman

~~~~~~~~~~~~~

Our problem in the immediate future will not be the lack of opportunities for the really motivated, but the lack of motivated people ready and able to take advantage of the opportunities.

>—Author Unknown

~~~~~~~~~~~~~

A sense of humor is part of the art of leadership, of getting along with people, of getting things done.

>—Dwight D. Eisenhower

~~~~~~~~~~~~~

Integrity is honesty carried through the fibers of the being and the whole mind, into thought as well as action so that the person is complete in honesty. That kind of integrity I put above all else as an essential of leadership.

>—Pearl S. Buck, Author,
>Missionary in China

We all need a sense of humor or someday we will wake up with no sense at all.

—Melvin Helitzer,
Author, Humorist

———————————

I was seldom able to see an opportunity until it had ceased to be one.

—Mark Twain

———————————

Our greatest weakness lies in giving up. The most certain way to succeed is always to try one more time.

—Thomas Edison

———————————

Vision is not necessarily having a plan, but having a mind that always plans. In sum, vision means to be in touch with the unlimited potential and expanse of this marvelous instrument called the human mind.

—Peter Koestenbaum,
Author, Businessman

———————————

A professional is one who does his best when he feels the least like working.

—Frank Lloyd Wright

———————————

If you want to be successful, it's just this simple: Know what you're doing. Love what you're doing. And believe in what you're doing.

—O. A. Battista, Author

If people are coming to work excited, if they're making mistakes freely and fearlessly, if they're having fun, if they're concentrating on doing things, rather than preparing reports and going to meetings—then somewhere you have a leader.

—Robert Townsend,
Author

To be a leader means willingness to risk—and a willingness to love. Has the leader given you something from the heart?

—Hubert Humphrey

It's never too late to be what you might have been.

—George Ernst, Author

You can't build your reputation on what you're going to do.

—Henry Ford

There are countless ways of attaining greatness, but any road to reaching one's maximum potential must be built on a bedrock of respect for the individual, a commitment to excellence, and a rejection of mediocrity.

—Author Unknown

SUCCESS

Try not to become a man of
success, but rather a man
of value.

—*Albert Einstein*

Success is getting what you want. Happiness is liking what you get.

> —H. Jackson Brown,
> Author

Success is not the result of spontaneous combustion. You must first set yourself on fire.

> —Fred Shero,
> Ice Hockey Coach

Do not let what you cannot do interfere with what you can do.

> —John Wooden,
> Basketball Coach

The three great essentials to achieve anything worthwhile are, first, hard work, second, stick-to-it-iveness, third, common sense.

> —Thomas Edison

Somehow I can't believe that there are any heights that can't be scaled by a man who knows the secrets of making dreams come true. This special secret, it seems to me, can be summarized in four C's. They are curiosity, confidence, courage, and constancy; and the greatest of all is confidence.

> —Walt Disney

Some people dream of worthy accomplishments, while others stay awake and do them.

—Constance Newman,
Diplomat

Ability is what you're capable of doing. Motivation determines what you do. Attitude determines how well you do it.

—Lou Holtz,
Football Coach

Success is going from failure to failure without loss of enthusiasm.

—Winston Churchill

To become successful you must be a person of action. Merely to "know" is not sufficient. It is necessary to both know and do.

—Napoleon Hill, Author,
Motivational Speaker

Apply yourself. Get all the education you can, but then, by God, do something. Don't just stand there, make it happen.

—Lee Iaccoca, Author,
Businessman

Hold your head high, stick your chest out. You can make it. It gets dark sometimes but morning comes. Keep hope alive.

—Rev. Jesse Jackson

~~~~~~~~~~~~

Success comes from knowing that you did your best to become the best that you are capable of becoming.

—John Wooden,
Basketball Coach

~~~~~~~~~~~~

There is only one other lesson that success should teach us. Be as amazed by your own success as your friends are.

—Harvey Mackay,
Author, Motivational Speaker

~~~~~~~~~~~~

Success comes in cans; failure comes in can'ts.

—Author Unknown

~~~~~~~~~~~~

For success, attitude is equally as important as ability.

—Harry F. Banks, Author

On Being Yourself:
You have brains in your head.
You have feet in your shoes.
You can steer yourself any direction you choose.
You're on your own.
And you know what you know.
And YOU are the guy who'll decide where to go.

—Dr. Seuss

———————————————

The price of success is hard work, dedication to the job at hand, and the determination that whether we win or lose, we have applied the best of ourselves to the task at hand.

—Vince Lombardi,
Football Coach

———————————————

Success is courageously living each moment as fully as possible. Success means the courage to flow, struggle, change, grow, and all other contradictions of the human condition. Success means being true to you.

—Tom Rusk and
Randy Read, Authors

———————————————

I don't want to get to the end of my life and find that I just lived the length of it. I want to have lived the width of it as well.

—Diane Ackerman, Poet

Tomorrow is the most important thing in life. It comes to us at midnight very clean. It's perfect when it arrives, and it puts itself in our hands and hopes we've learned something from yesterday.

—John Wayne

Life is an adventure of passion, risk, danger, laughter, beauty, love, a burning curiosity to go with the action to see what it is all about, to search for a pattern of meaning, to burn one's bridges because you're never going to go back anyway, and to live to the end.

—Saul Alinsky,
Political Activist

Success is finding and doing to the best of your ability, in each moment of your life, what you enjoy most doing, what you can do best, and what has the greatest possibility of providing the means to live as you would like to live in relation to yourself and the persons you value.

—Nido Qubein, Author,
Motivational Speaker

Values are the foundation of our character and of our confidence. A person who does not know what he stands for or what he should stand for will never enjoy true happiness and success.

—Lionel Kendrick, Author

*The rung of a ladder was never meant to rest upon,
but only to hold a man's foot long enough to
enable him to put the other somewhat higher.*

—Thomas Huxley,
Biologist

———————————

Don't compromise yourself. You are all you've got.

—Betty Ford,
Former First Lady

———————————

*More important than being successful is being
significant. Significance means making a
contribution to others.*

—Stephen Covey,
Author, Motivational Speaker

———————————

*If you have the will to win, you have achieved half
your success. If you don't, you have achieved half
your failure.*

—David Ambrose,
Author

———————————

*If you have made mistakes, there is always another
chance for you. You may have a fresh start any
moment you choose, for this thing we call "failure"
is not the falling down, but the staying down.*

—Mary Pickford, Actress

Since it doesn't cost a dime to dream, you'll never shortchange yourself when you stretch your imagination.

> —Robert Schuller,
> Minister, Crystal Cathedral

When you aim for perfection, you discover it's a moving target.

> —George Fisher, Author

The great secret to success is to go through life as a man who never gets used up.

> —Albert Schweitzer,
> Humanitarian,
> Missionary

Some of the world's greatest feats were accomplished by people not smart enough to know that they were impossible.

> —Doug Larson,
> Cartoonist

Winners make goals; losers make excuses.

> —Author Unknown

If you do not think about the future, you cannot have one.

—John Galsworthy,
Nobel Prize-Winning Author

Commitment is the enemy of resistance, for it is the serious promise to press on, to get up, no matter how many times you are knocked down.

—David McNally,
Author, Motivational Speaker

Consider how hard it is to change yourself, and you'll understand what little chance you have of trying to change others.

—Jacob Braude, Author

Motivation is a fire from within. If someone else tries to light that fire under you, chances are it will burn very briefly.

—Stephen Covey,
Author, Motivational Speaker

The way I see it, if you want the rainbow, you gotta put up with the rain.

—Dolly Parton,
Singer, Songwriter

An individual's self-concept is the core of his personality. It affects every aspect of human behavior: the ability to learn, the capacity to grow and change, the choice of friends, mates and careers. It is no exaggeration to say that a strong positive self-image is the best possible preparation for success in life.

—Dr. Joyce Brothers,
Psychologist

People are always blaming their circumstances. I don't believe in circumstances. People who get on in this world are the people who get up and look for the circumstances they want, and if they can't find them, make them.

—George Bernard Shaw,
Playwright

Luke, there is no try, there is either do or not do.

—Yoda,
The Empire Strikes Back

Belief is the knowledge that we can do something. It's the inner feeling that what we undertake, we can accomplish. For the most part, all of us have the ability to look at something and know whether or not we can do it. So, in belief there is power: our eyes are opened; our opportunities becomes plain; our visions become realities.

—Author Unknown

We can only do what we think we can do. We can be only what we think we can be. We can have only what we think we can have. What we do, what we are, what we have, all depend upon what we think.

—Robert Collier, Author

~~~~~~~~~~~~~~~~

Success in life has nothing to do with what you gain in life or accomplish for yourself. It's what you do for others.

—Danny Thomas,
Actor, Comedian

~~~~~~~~~~~~~~~~

You are free to choose, but the choices you make today will determine what you will have, be and do in the tomorrow of your life.

—Zig Ziglar,
Author, Motivational Speaker

~~~~~~~~~~~~~~~~

To see things in the seed, that is genius.

—Lao-Tzu

~~~~~~~~~~~~~~~~

There are no secrets to success. It is the result of preparation, hard work, and learning from failure.

—General Colin Powell

Spread your arms to those with needs, and serve
     with joy and zest;
Fill each day with golden deeds, and give your
     very best.

—William A. Ward,
Author

Success doesn't come to you; you go to it.

—Marva Collins,
School Principal

Some men succeed because they are destined
to, but most men succeed because they are
determined to.

—Author Unknown

The business of expanding your consciousness is
not an option. Either you are expandable or you are
expendable.

—Robert Schuller,
Minister, Crystal Cathedral

So you've got a problem? That's good! Why?
Because repeated victories over your problems are
the rungs on your ladder to success. With each
victory you grow in wisdom, stature and experience.
You become a bigger, better, more successful person

each time you meet a problem and tackle and
conquer it with a positive mental attitude.

—Mark Twain

Your life is the sum result of all the choices you
make, both consciously and unconsciously. If you
can control the process of choosing, you can
take control of all aspects of your life. You can find
the freedom that comes from being in charge of
yourself.

—Robert Service, Poet

Don't aim at success—the more you aim at it and
make it a target, the more you are going to miss it.
For success, like happiness, cannot be pursued;
it must ensue, as the unintended side effect of
one's personal dedication to a course greater than
oneself.

—Viktor Frankl, Author,
Holocaust Survivor

Our beliefs about what we are and what we can be
precisely determine what we will be.

—Anthony Robbins,
Author, Motivational Speaker

The only thing that stands between a man and what he wants from life is often merely the will to try it and the faith to believe that it is possible.

—Richard De Vos,
Author

———————

Success has a price tag on it, and the tag reads "Courage, Determination, Discipline, Risk Taking, Perseverance, and Consistency"—doing the right things for the right reasons and not just when we feel like it.

—James Meston, Author

———————

The ultimate of being successful is the luxury of giving yourself the time to do what you want to do.

—Leontyne Price,
Opera Singer

———————

In life you are given two ends, one to think with and the other to sit on. Your success in life depends on which end you use the most. Heads you win, tails you lose.

—Conrad Burns,
U.S. Senator, Montana

11

COMMUNICATION

The biggest problem with communication is the illusion that it has taken place.

George Bernard Shaw

The real art of communication is not only to say the right thing in the right place, but to leave unsaid the wrong thing at the tempting moment.

—Dorothy Nevill, Writer

~~~~~~~~~~

If you say what you think, don't expect to hear only what you like.

—Malcolm Forbes,
Publisher

~~~~~~~~~~

It's hard to listen when you're planning something you think needs to be said.

—Author Unknown

~~~~~~~~~~

Most conversations are monologues delivered in the presence of a witness.

—Margaret Miller,
Author

~~~~~~~~~~

Courage is what it takes to stand up and speak—courage is also what it takes to sit down and listen.

—Winston Churchill

Friends are those rare people who ask how we are and then wait to hear the answer.

—Ed Cunningham,
Author

Many people who have the gift of gab don't know how to wrap it up.

—Arnold Glasow, Author

Too often we enjoy the comfort of opinion without the discomfort of thought.

—John F. Kennedy

Put it before them briefly so they will read it, clearly so they will appreciate it, picturesquely so they will remember it and, above all, accurately so they will be guided by its light.

—Joseph Pulitzer,
Journalist, Publisher

While listening may be the most undervalued of all the communication skills, good people managers are likely to listen more than they speak. Perhaps that's why God gave us two ears and only one mouth.

—Mary Kay Ash,
Businesswoman
(Mary Kay Cosmetics)

It doesn't matter what you intend to communicate, but how it's heard that counts.

　　　　　　　　　　　　—Author Unknown

Communication does not begin with being understood, but with understanding.

　　　　　　　　　　　　—W. Steven Brown,
　　　　　　　　　　　　Author

There are two types of people—those who come into a room and say, "Well, here I am!" and those who come in and say, "Ah, there you are."

　　　　　　　　　　　　—Frederick L. Collins,
　　　　　　　　　　　　Author

Words have a magical power. They can bring either the greatest happiness or deepest despair; they can transfer knowledge from teacher to student; words enable the orator to sway his audience and dictate its decision. Words are capable of arousing the strongest emotions and prompting all men's actions.

　　　　　　　　　　　　—Sigmund Freud

In order that all men may be taught to speak the truth, it is necessary that all likewise should learn to hear it.

　　　　　　　　　　　　—Samuel Johnson

Precision of communication is important, more important than ever, in our era of hair-trigger balances, when a false or misunderstood word may create as much disaster as a sudden thoughtless act.

—James Thurber,
Author, Humorist

People love to talk but hate to listen. Listening is not merely not talking, though even that is beyond most of our powers; it means taking a vigorous, human interest in what is being told us. You can listen like a brick wall or like a splendid auditorium where every sound comes back fuller and richer.

—Alice Duer Miller,
Author

The greatest gift you can give another is the purity of your attention.

—Richard Moss,
Author, Seminar Leader

Silences regulate the flow of listening and talking. They are to conversation what zeroes are to mathematics—crucial nothings without which communication can't work.

—Author Unknown

Man does not live by words alone, despite the fact that sometimes he has to eat them.

—Adlai Stevenson

I know you believe you understand what you think I said, but I am not sure you realize that what you heard is not what I meant.

—Author Unknown

The greatest compliment that was ever paid to me was when someone asked me what I thought, and attended to my answer.

—Henry David Thoreau

The right word may be effective, but no word was ever as effective as a rightly timed pause.

—Mark Twain

The most important thing in communication is to hear what isn't being said.

—Peter Drucker, Author

12

BALANCING THE TIME CRUNCH

If we are ever to enjoy life,
now is the time—not
tomorrow or next year. The
best preparation for a
better life next year is a
full, complete, harmonious,
joyous life this year.

—*Thomas Drier, Author*

Don't say you don't have enough time. You have exactly the same number of hours per day that were given to Helen Keller, Pasteur, Michaelangelo, Mother Teresa, Leonardo da Vinci, Thomas Jefferson, and Albert Einstein.

—H. Jackson Brown Jr.,
Author

Imagine life as a game in which you are juggling some five balls in the air. You name them work, family, health, friends, and spirit—and you're keeping all of these in the air. You will soon understand that work is a rubber ball. If you drop it, it will bounce back. But the other four balls— family, health, friends, and spirit are made of glass. If you drop one of these, they will be irrevocably scuffed, marked, nicked, damaged, or even shattered. They will never be the same. You must understand that and strive for balance in your life.

—Brian Dyson,
Coca-Cola Executive

We live in constant tension between the urgent and the important. The problem is that the important tasks rarely must be done today, or even this week. But urgent tasks call for instant action—endless demands pressure every hour of the day. The momentary appeal of these urgent tasks seems irresistible and important, and they devour our energy. But in the light of time's perspective their deceptive prominence fades; with a sense of loss we recall the important tasks pushed aside. We realize we've become slaves to the tyranny of the urgent.

—Charles Hummel,
Author

———————

One of the characteristics of effective leaders is that they continually find joy in their jobs. This gives them the energy to energize others. They maintain a positive outlook and avoid burnout by focusing on what's right rather than what's wrong, constantly learning and growing on the job, making friends with problems, picking the right dance partners (associating with winners), keeping their sense of humor and getting a life outside of work.

—Robert Ramsey,
Educator, Author

———————

There is more to life than increasing its speed.

—Mahatma Gandhi

———————

Talking about balancing work and life really applies to all of us, not just teachers. The main message is if you pay attention to the non-work side of things, you will be better at work. So to be better at life is to be better at work. To be better at work by itself will not last very long. It will eventually take its toll. And if people pay attention to both sides of each other, it will be better.

—Michael Fullan,
Educator, Author

Time is a versatile performer. It flies, marches on, heals all wounds, runs out, and will tell.

—Franklin P. Jones,
Author

———————

Leaders set aside a portion of each day (even if it's only a matter of minutes) for quiet time devoted to prayer, meditation, imaging, or just daydreaming. Quietude is an elixir that every leader needs.

—Robert Ramsey,
Educator, Author

———————

How simple it is to see that all the worry in the world cannot control the future. How simple it is to see that we can only be happy now. And that there will never be a time when it is not now.

—Gerald Jampolsky,
Author, Psychiatrist

———————

Time is what we want most but what we use worst.

—William Penn,
Statesman

———————

Stress: When your heart is in one place and your body is in another.

—Author Unknown

He who every morning plans the transaction of the day and follows out that plan, carries a thread that will guide him through the maze of the most busy life. But, where no plain is laid, where the disposal of time is surrendered merely to the chance of incidence, chaos will soon reign.

—Victor Hugo

~~~~~~~~~~~~

Learn to value your time alone—when you value something you are keener to protect it.

—Author Unknown

~~~~~~~~~~~~

Inside myself is a place where I live all alone and that's where you renew your springs that never dry up.

—Pearl Buck, Author,
Missionary in China

~~~~~~~~~~~~

No one can see his reflection in running water but only in still water. Only that which is itself still can still the seekers of stillness.

—Chuang Tzu,
Taoist Philosopher

~~~~~~~~~~~~

It is who is in your life that matters, not what is your life.

—Author Unknown

We're getting more done in less time, but where are the rich relationships, the inner peace, the balance, the confidence that we're doing what matters most and doing it well?

—Author Unknown

The main thing is to keep the main thing the main thing.

—Stephen Covey,
Author, Motivational Speaker

Too bad most of us postpone goofing off until Saturday or Sunday. In doing so, we put pressure on the weekend. Procrastinating on schedule is creating another form of obligation. So try to waste time on the spur of the moment, on a Wednesday, or a Thursday. Later—much later—when you get the hang of it, you'll be able to show off and fritter time away on a Monday.

—Veronique Vienne,
Author

Live each day as you would climb a mountain. An occasional glance towards the summit keeps the goal in mind, but many beautiful scenes are to be observed from each new vantage point. So climb slowly, enjoying each passing moment; and then the view from the summit will serve a more rewarding climax for your journey.

—Bishop Fulton Sheen

We're constantly caught up in "the thick of thin things"—putting out fires and never making time to do what we know would make a difference.

> —Stephen Covey,
> Author, Motivational Speaker

————————

Time isn't the enemy. It's not an obstacle or an unfair restraint. Time is a working condition. It is a tool. Time is a resource much like money. Time can be counted, budgeted, spent, and even squandered, but it can't be invested to earn interest. Time can't grow. It can only shrink. Time plays no favorites. Everyone gets the same amount to start with. What he or she does with it is up to each individual. Leaders don't have more time than anyone else. They just make better use of their time on and off the job. Time management is simply making choices. Better choices mean better time use.

> —Robert Ramsey,
> Educator, Author

————————

You must constantly guard against the trap of falling into a routine of remaining busy with unimportant chores that will provide you with an excuse to avoid meaningful challenges or opportunities that could change your life for the better.

> —Og Mandino, Author

The most wasted day of all is that on which we have not laughed.

> —Sebastien Chamfort,
> French Playwright

There's never enough time to do it right but there's always enough time to do it over.

> —Jack Bergman,
> Marketing Consultant

Leaders devote time every day to tipping the scale toward a more balanced life. This means taking care of themselves (exercising, resting properly, eating right); nurturing friendships; spending time with family members; nourishing the spirit; and having fun. If you can't find or make time for these activities, you're not the leader of the organization. You're a slave to it.

> —Robert Ramsey,
> Educator, Author

Things which matter most must never be done at the mercy of things which matter least.

> —Goethe

Hard work is often the easy work you did not do at the proper time.

> —Bernard Meltzer,
> Law Professor

Many things which cannot be overcome when they stand together yield themselves up when taken little by little.

—Sertorius,
Roman Statesman

I have learned, and it's been a hard lesson, that the more time I take to be still, sometimes introspective, or just to catch my breath, the better my next task is completed. I get better results when I make the pauses as meaningful as the battle.

—Jonathon Lazear,
Author, Publisher

If your nose is close to the grindstone and you hold it there long enough, in time you'll say there's no such thing as brooks that babble and birds that sing. These three will all your world compose: Just you, the stone, and your poor old nose.

—Inscription on a
200-year-old Gravestone

I can complain because the rose bush has thorns or rejoice because the thornbush has roses.

—Author Unknown

We still do not know one-thousandth of one percent of what nature has revealed to us.

—Albert Einstein

Doing nothing requires no prior skills, no personal trainers, no exercise machines, and no financial commitment. All you need to do is change your way of thinking. Instead of rushing around from task to task, always worrying about what's next, grant yourself permission to linger in the moment.

> —Veronique Vienne,
> Author

Having time is absolutely essential. You need time to think. You need time to "be" with your thoughts, to mull them over, to change them again until you light upon the right thoughts that will guide you where you want to go. You need time to figure out where you are—with a project you're in the middle of, with the direction your career is headed, with the course your life is taking. It's because we haven't had time to think that we've allowed our work lives to get so out of control.

> —Elaine St. James,
> Author

Finding a way to live the simple life is today's most complicated problem.

> —Jimmy Townsend,
> Author

Love and time—those are the only two things in all the world and all of life that cannot be bought, but only spent.

> —Gary Jennings,
> Novelist

History has demonstrated that the most notable winners usually encountered heartbreaking obstacles before they triumphed. They finally won because they refused to become discouraged by their defeats. Disappointments acted as a challenge. Don't let difficulties discourage you.

—B. C. Forbes, Publisher

He has achieved success who has lived well, laughed often, and loved much; who has gained the respect of intelligent men and the love of children; who has filled his niche and accomplished his task; who leaves the world better than he found it, whether by an improved poppy, a perfect poem, or a rescued soul; who never lacked appreciation of earth's beauty or failed to express it; who looked for the best in others and gave them the best he had; whose life was an inspiration; whose memory a benediction.

—Bessie Stanley,
Housewife, Essayist

The great dividing line between success and failure can be expressed in 5 words: "I did not have time."

—Robert Hastings,
Author

I resolve to live with all my might while I do live. I resolve never to lose one moment of time and to improve my use of time in the most profitable way I possibly can. I resolve never to do anything I wouldn't do, if it were the last hour of my life.

—Jonathan Edwards,
Theologian

Leadership and planning go together. Leaders plan—period! They don't wait for time to plan. They don't complain about not having time for planning. They don't make excuses for not planning. They simply and systematically set aside time to dream about the future, envision possibilities, project and extrapolate, predict, set goals, outline strategies, and establish timelines. That's called planning. It's what all good leaders do.

—Robert Ramsey,
Educator, Author

May we never let the things we can't have, or don't have, or shouldn't have, spoil our enjoyment of the things we do have and can have. As we value our happiness, let us not forget it, for one of the greatest lessons in life is learning to be happy without the things we cannot or should not have.

—Richard Evans, Author

Become aware of the endless stream of paper that flows into your life on a daily basis that keeps you from concentrating on what's truly important. We spend untold hours: taking it in; glancing at it; sorting through it; reading it; stacking it on a corner of the desk; glancing through it again; setting it aside; then later trying to find it again; not knowing what to do with it; finally deciding what to do with it; filing it; passing it on to clutter up someone else's space; setting it aside to clutter up our own space; or tossing it out.

—Elaine St. James,
Author

People forget how fast you did a job—but they remember how well you did it.

> —Howard Newton,
> Composer

The present is the point at which time touches eternity.

> —C. S. Lewis

Time is the scarcest resource and unless it is managed, nothing else can be managed.

> —Peter Drucker, Author

What is the true picture of your life? Imagine that there is an hourglass on your desk. Connecting the bowl at the top with the bowl at the bottom is a tube so thin that only one grain of sand can pass through it at a time. That is the true picture of your life, even on a super-busy day. The crowded hours come to you always one moment at a time. That is the only way they can come. The day brings many tasks, problems, strains, but invariably they come in single file. You want to gain emotional poise? Remember the hour glass, the grains of sand dropping one at a time.

> —James Gordon Gilkey,
> Theologian

This time, like all times, is a very good time, if we but know what to do with it.

—Ralph Waldo Emerson

~~~~~~~~

No one I know ever looked back on his or her life and said, "I wish I had spent more time at work."

—Author Unknown

~~~~~~~~

Enjoy your own company. Learn to welcome solitude and work on your inner being—your character. Solitude allows you opportunity to think deep thoughts. To think about where you've been. To think about where you're going. To think about why you feel so strongly about certain issues. To think about how different your values are from those of other people you know. To think about what all people have in common. To question yourself about why you cling to bad habits. To praise yourself for your strengths. To challenge yourself to follow your dreams. Reflection and solitude feed the soul.

—Dianna Booher, Author

~~~~~~~~

All you have to do is pause to rest. Nature herself, when we let her, will take care of everything else. It's our impatience that spoils things.

—Moliere

I am humbled by my realization of the sacredness of the time we are given and stunned by our irreverence for the time we have.

—Paul Pearsall, Author,
Motivational Speaker

———————————

Normal day, let me be aware of the treasure you are. Let me learn from you, love you, savor you, bless you before you depart. Let me not pass you by in quest of some rare and perfect tomorrow. Let me hold you while I may, for it will not always be so. One day I shall dig my nails into the earth, or bury my face in the pillow, or stretch myself taut, or raise my hands to the sky, and want, more than all the world, your return.

—Mary Jean Irion,
Educator, Poet

———————————

You must learn to be still in the midst of activity and to be vibrantly alive in repose.

—Indira Gandhi

———————————

Enjoy the little things in life, for one day you may look back and realize that they were the big things.

—Author Unknown

With all the changes and challenges you face each day, there's never been a greater need to take the time to determine your priorities, and then with renewed focus, align your daily actions with your purpose or goals. Since you can't know it all or do it all, it's vital that you learn to take the time to contemplate what it is you need to know and what you need to do.

—John Blaydes,
Educator, Author,
Motivational Speaker

PEARLS OF WISDOM

The art of being wise is to know what to overlook.

—William James,
Novelist

Happiness is when what you think, what you say, and what you do are in harmony.

>— *Mahatma Gandhi*

One thing I know: the only ones among you who will be really happy are those who will have sought and found how to serve.

>— *Albert Schweitzer,*
>*Humanitarian, Missionary*

To know others is wisdom, to know oneself— enlightenment.

>— *Tao Te Ching,*
>*Chinese Philosopher*

In seeking wisdom, the first step is silence, the second listening, the third remembering, the fourth practicing, the fifth—teaching others.

>— *Ibn Gabirol,*
>*Jewish Poet, Philosopher*

You have to accept whatever comes and the only important thing is that you meet it with courage and with the best you have to give.

>— *Eleanor Roosevelt*

Kindness is more important than wisdom, and the recognition of this is the beginning of wisdom.

> —Theodore Rubin,
> Author, Psychoanalyst

It does not require many words to speak the truth.

> —Chief Joseph

The best things in life aren't things.

> —Art Buchwald,
> Journalist

Men often become what they believe themselves to be. If I believe I cannot do something, it makes me incapable of doing it. But when I believe I can, then I acquire the ability to do it even if I didn't have it in the beginning.

> —Mahatma Gandhi

The sure way to miss success is to miss the opportunity. Be fearless and bold in your actions. Know what you want and go for it.

> —Rupert McCall

Far and away the best prize that life has to offer is the chance to work hard at work worth doing.

—Theodore Roosevelt

In the end we will not remember the voices of our enemies, but the silence of our friends.

—Martin Luther King Jr.

Never insult an alligator until you've crossed the river.

—Cordell Hull,
Nobel Peace Prize Winner

An aim in life is the only fortune worth finding.

—Jacqueline Kennedy

Mistakes are part of the dues one pays for a full life.

—Sophia Loren, Actress

It is better to be boldly decisive and risk being wrong than to agonize at length and be right too late.

—Marilyn Moats Kennedy,
Author, Motivational Speaker

Those who are free of resentful thoughts surely find peace.

—Buddha

~~~~~~~~~~~~~

Be master of your petty annoyances and conserve your energies for the big, worthwhile things. It isn't the mountain ahead that wears you out—it's the grain of sand in your shoe.

—Robert Service, Poet

~~~~~~~~~~~~~

The last of the human freedoms is to choose one's attitude in any given set of circumstances.

—Victor Frankl,
Author, Holocaust Survivor

~~~~~~~~~~~~~

Use the stones that life throws at you to lay the foundations for your future.

—Author Unknown

~~~~~~~~~~~~~

Worry can drag yesterday's clouds over today's sunshine.

—John Blaydes,
Educator, Author,
Motivational Speaker

There's only a slight difference between keeping
your chin up and sticking your neck out, but it's a
difference worth knowing.

—Author Unknown

Those who hate you don't win unless you hate
them—and then you destroy yourself.

—Richard Nixon

A pint of example is worth a gallon of advice.

—Author Unknown

I have found that if you love life, life will
love you back. I accept life unconditionally. Life
holds so much—so much to be happy about
always.

—Author Unknown

Most people ask for happiness on condition.
Happiness can be felt only if you don't set
conditions.

—Arthur Rubinstein,
Pianist

He that gives good advice, builds with one hand;
he that gives good counsel and example, builds
with both.

—Francis Bacon

~~~~~~~~~~~~~~~

Enthusiasm is the match that ignites the candle of
achievement.

—Author Unknown

~~~~~~~~~~~~~~~

Have the courage to say no. Have the courage to
face the truth. Do the right thing because it is
right. These are the magic keys to living your life
with integrity.

—Mark Twain

~~~~~~~~~~~~~~~

Life is not a destination; it's a journey. It's not a
series of goals; it's a series of steps, of events
unfolding as you make your way.

—Author Unknown

~~~~~~~~~~~~~~~

Life is not about accomplishment; it's all about
doing, participating, progressing, growing, learning.

—Mike Hernacki, Author

The purpose of life, after all, is to live it, to taste experience to the utmost, to reach out eagerly and without fear for newer and richer experiences.

— *Eleanor Roosevelt*

Sometimes our light goes out but is blown into flame by another human being. Each of us owes deepest thanks to those who have rekindled this light.

— *Albert Schweitzer,*
Humanitarian, Missionary

The man who does not read good books
has no advantage over the man who can't
read them.

— *Mark Twain*

One of the lessons of history is that nothing is often a good thing to do and always a clever thing to say.

— *Will Durant,*
Author, Historian

By three methods we may learn wisdom: first, by reflection, which is noblest; second, by imitation, which is easiest; and third, by experience, which is the bitterest.

—Confucius

14
CREATING A CULTURE OF EXCELLENCE

We hold these truths to be self-evident, that all men are created equal, that they are endowed by their Creator with certain inalienable rights, that among these are life, liberty, and the pursuit of happiness.

—*Declaration of Independence*

Measurement is the first step that leads to control and eventually to improvement. If you can't measure something, you can't understand it. If you can't understand it, you can't control it. If you can't control it, you can't improve it.

—H. James Harrington,
Author

_____

Trust men and they will be true to you; treat them greatly and they will show themselves great.

—Ralph Waldo Emerson

_____

Excellence in education is the key to our nation's future. We must empower all our students with the best schools and guidance possible if we are truly to prepare for the challenges of tomorrow. At a time when we face stark choices about how best to strengthen our economic future, our commitment to education and to children must stand absolutely firm. We have a sacred obligation to put children's needs first and to make the essential investments that will help them to succeed.

—Bill Clinton

_____

First make sure that what you aspire to accomplish is worth accomplishing, and then throw your whole vitality into it. What's worth doing is worth doing well. And to do anything well, whether it be typing a letter or drawing up an agreement involving millions, we must give not only our hands to the

doing of it, but our brains, our enthusiasm, the all
that is in us. The task to which you dedicate
yourself can never become a drudgery.

—B. C. Forbes, Publisher

~~~~~~~~~

There are risks and costs to a program of action.
But they are far less than the long-range risks and
costs of a comfortable inaction.

—John F. Kennedy

~~~~~~~~~

When we become conditioned to perceived truth
and closed to new possibilities, the following
happens: We see what we expect to see, not what
we can see. We hear what we expect to hear, not
what we can hear. We think what we expect to
think, not what we can think.

—John C. Maxwell,
Author, Minister

~~~~~~~~~

Example is not the main thing in influencing others.
It is the only thing.

—Albert Schweitzer,
Humanitarian, Missionary

~~~~~~~~~

Conflict is inevitable, but combat is optional.

—Max Lucado,
Author, Minister

I truly believe we should never give up our hopes and dreams. The path may be rocky and twisted, but the world is waiting for that special contribution that each of us was born to make. What it takes is the courage to follow the whispers of wisdom that guide us from the inside. When I listen to that, I expect nothing less than a miracle.

—Marilyn Johnson Kondwani,
Author

If a·man is called to be a streetsweeper, he should sweep streets even as Michelangelo painted, or Beethoven composed music, or Shakespeare wrote poetry. He should sweep streets so well that all the hosts of heaven and earth will pause to say, here lived a great streetsweeper who did his job well.

—Martin Luther King Jr.

Excellence is a journey, not a place to be.

—Author Unknown

First-rate people hire first-rate people, second-rate people hire third-rate people.

—Leo Rosten, Author

In the long run you hit only what you aim at. Therefore, though you should fail immediately, you had better aim at something high.

—Henry David Thoreau

The purpose of goals is to focus our attention. The mind will not reach toward achievement until it has clear objectives. The magic begins when we set goals. It is then that the switch is turned on, the current begins to flow, and the power to accomplish becomes a reality.

—From The Best of
Success newsletter,
compiled by Wyn Davis

Some people may have greatness thrust upon them. Very few have excellence thrust upon them. They achieve it. They do not achieve it unwittingly, by doin' what comes naturally, and they don't stumble into it in the course of amusing themselves. All excellence involves discipline and tenacity of purpose.

—John Gardner, Author

Enthusiasm is the electric current that keeps the engine of life going at top speed. Enthusiasm is the very propeller of progress.

—B.C. Forbes, Publisher

If civilization is to survive, we must cultivate the science of human relationships, the ability of all peoples, of all kinds, to live together, in the same world at peace.

—Franklin D. Roosevelt

Be brave enough to live creatively. The creative is the place where no one else has ever been. You have to leave the city of your comfort and go into the wilderness of your intuition. You can't get there by bus, only by hard work, risking, and by not quite knowing what you're doing. What you'll discover will be wonderful: yourself.

—Alan Alda, Actor

You cannot help men permanently by doing for them what they could do and should do for themselves.

—Abraham Lincoln

Excellence is not a matter of chance; it's a matter of choice. It's not a thing to be waited for, it's a thing to be achieved.

—Author Unknown

Unless we come apart and rest a while, we may just come apart.

—Vance Havner,
Author, Minister

Well done is better than well said.

—Benjamin Franklin

The secret of joy is contained in one word—excellence. To know how to do something well is to enjoy it.

—Pearl S. Buck, Author,
Missionary to China

*Excellence is to do a common thing in an
uncommon way.*

> —Booker T. Washington,
>   Educator, Black Rights
>   Leader

---

*Excellence resides in quality, not quantity. The best
is always few and rare; much lowers value.*

> —Gracian,
>   Spanish Philosopher, Writer

---

*If you want to get the best out of a man, you must
look for the best that is in him.*

> —Bernard Haldane,
>   Businessman, Career Management

---

*In the absence of a vision, there can be no clear
and consistent focus. In the absence of a dream,
there can be no renewal of hope. In the absence of
a philosophy, there is no real meaning to work and
to life itself.*

> —Joe Batten, Author,
>   Motivational Speaker

15

ENCOURAGEMENT FOR THE SOUL

Kind words can be short
and easy to speak, but
their echoes are truly
endless.

—Mother Teresa

*Nothing improves a person's hearing more than praise.
An ounce of praise can accomplish more than a ton of
faultfinding. And if one looks for it, something worthy
of praise can be found in every child.*

—John Drescher, Author

*If you have some respect for people as they are,
you can be more effective in helping them to
become better than they are.*

—John Gardner, Author

A laugh is a smile that bursts.

—Mary Waldrip, Author

*There is something that is much more scarce,
something rarer than ability. It is the ability to
recognize ability.*

—Robert Half,
Businessman, Recruiting Services

*Plant the seeds of expectation in your mind;
cultivate thoughts that anticipate achievement.
Believe in yourself as being capable of overcoming
all obstacles and weaknesses.*

—Norman Vincent Peale,
Author, Minister

Nothing else can quite substitute for a few well-chosen, well-timed, sincere words of praise. They're absolutely free—and worth a fortune.

> —Sam Walton,
> Businessman
> (Wal Mart)

———————

There are two things people want more than sex and money—recognition and praise.

> —Mary Kay Ash,
> Businesswoman
> (Mary Kay Cosmetics)

———————

Human beings, like plants, grow in the soil of acceptance, not in the atmosphere of rejection.

> —John Powell, Author

———————

Catch them doing something right! If you can catch people doing something well, no matter how small it may seem, and positively reinforce them for doing it, they will continue to grow in a positive direction.

> —Ken Blanchard, Author

———————

There are high spots in all of our lives and most of them come about through encouragement from someone else. Encouragement is oxygen for the soul.

> —George Matthew Adams,
> Author

Kindness put off until tomorrow may become only a bitter regret.

—Author Unknown

We shall never know all the good that a simple smile can do.

—Mother Teresa

Treat people as if they were what they ought to be and you help them become what they are capable of being.

—Goethe

A desire to be observed, considered, esteemed, praised, beloved, and admired by his fellows is one of the earliest as well as the keenest dispositions discovered in the heart of man.

—John Adams

In the time we have, it is surely our duty to do all the good we can to all the people we can in all the ways we can.

—William Barclay,
Theologian

Let me be a little kinder, let me be a little blinder to the faults of those around me.

—Edward Guest, Author

*Beginning today, treat everyone you meet
as if they were going to be dead by midnight.
Extend to them all the care, kindness, and
understanding you can muster, and do it with no
thought of any reward. Your life will never be the
same again.*

—Og Mandino, Author,
Motivational Speaker

*The time for action is now. It's never too late to do
something.*

—Carl Sandburg, Poet

Be kind to unkind people—they need it the most.

—Author Unknown

*Tranquility can be reached by simply allowing the
mind to become quiet.*

—Author Unknown

*From tranquility emerges a person brimming over
with self-reliance and contentment.*

—Author Unknown

The dream begins, most of the time, with a teacher who believes in you, who tugs and pushes and leads you on to the next plateau, sometimes poking you with a sharp stick called truth.

—Dan Rather,
Broadcast Journalist

—————————————

Silent gratitude isn't very much use to anyone.

—G. B. Stern, Author

—————————————

I expect to pass through life but once. If therefore, there be any kindness I can show or any good things I can do to fellow human beings, let me do it now, and not defer or neglect it, as I shall not pass this way again.

—William Penn

—————————————

People do not live by bread alone. They need buttering up once in awhile.

—Robert Henry,
Author (Robert's Rules of Order)

—————————————

We all need it. The deepest principle in human nature is the craving to be appreciated.

—William James, Author

Too often we underestimate the power of a touch, a smile, a kind word, a listening ear, an honest compliment, or the smallest act of caring, all of which have the potential to turn a life around.

—Leo Buscaglia, Author

A smile costs nothing but gives much. It enriches those who receive without making poorer those who give. It takes but a moment, but the memory of it sometimes lasts forever. None is so rich or mighty that he can get along without it, and none is so poor that he cannot be made rich by it. A smile creates happiness in the home, fosters goodwill in business and is the countersign of friendship. It brings rest to the weary, cheer to the discouraged, sunshine to the sad, and is nature's best antidote for trouble. Yet it cannot be bought, begged or borrowed, or stolen, for it is something that is of no value to anyone until it is given away. Some people are too tired to give you a smile. Give them one of yours, as none needs a smile so much as he who has not more to give.

—Author Unknown

EDUCATION IS THE KEY

There are people who learn, who are open to what happens around them, who listen, who hear the lessons. When they do something stupid, they don't do it again. And when they do something that works a little bit, they do it even better and harder the next time. The question to ask is not whether you are a success or a failure, but whether you are a learner or non-learner.

—*Benjamin Barber,*
Author, Political Theorist

All of us do not have equal talent, but all of us should have an equal opportunity to develop our talents.

—John F. Kennedy

It will be a great day in education when schools have all the money they need and the air force will have to hold a bake sale to raise funds for a bomber.

—Women's International
League for Peace and
Freedom

Education is learning what you didn't even know you didn't know.

—Daniel Boorstin,
Author, Historian

The school is the last expenditure upon which America should be willing to economize.

—Franklin D. Roosevelt

Education is what's left over after you have forgotten everything you learned in school.

—Albert Einstein

Nine-tenths of education is encouragement.

> —Anatole France,
> Nobel Prize-Winning Author

~~~~~~~~~~~

Education's purpose is to replace an empty mind with an open one.

> —Malcolm Forbes,
> Publisher

~~~~~~~~~~~

Bear in mind that the wonderful things you learn in your schools are the work of many generations. All this is put in your hands as your inheritance in order that you may receive it, honor it, add to it, and one day faithfully hand it on to your children.

> —Albert Einstein

~~~~~~~~~~~

The essence of our effort to see that every child has a chance must be to assure each an equal opportunity, not to become equal, but to become different—to realize whatever unique potential of body, mind and spirit he or she possesses.

> —John Fischer, Author

~~~~~~~~~~~

As for me, all I know is that I know nothing.

> —Socrates

A graduation ceremony is an event where the commencement speaker tells thousands of students dressed in identical caps and gowns that individuality is the key to success.

—Bob Orben,
Author, Humorist

Try this sometime. Get a group of children in a room with a light fixture hanging just out of their grasp. Then watch what happens: one child will jump to touch it, and before you know it, every kid in the room will be leaping like Michael Jordan. They're testing their skills, stimulated by the challenge of reaching something beyond their normal grasp. Put the same children in a room where everything is easily in reach, there will be no jumping, no competition, no challenges. The problem with American education is a low ceiling of expectations. We have built schools that demand and teach too little, and the children have stopped jumping.

—Carroll Campbell,
Governor of South Carolina

Education is our passport to the future, for tomorrow belongs to the people who prepare for it today.

—Malcolm X, Author,
Civil Rights Activist

The secret of education lies in respecting the pupil.

—Ralph Waldo Emerson

The primary purpose of goal setting is to pull change in the direction you have chosen—one which fits your expertise and overall plan.

—Author Unknown

Education is forcing abstract ideas into concrete heads.

—Author Unknown

The aim of education should be to convert the mind into a living fountain and not a reservoir. That which is filled by merely pumping in, will be emptied by pumping out.

—John M. Mason,
Author

Education is a progressive discovery of our own ignorance.

—Will Durant,
Author, Historian

A little learning is a dangerous thing, but a lot of ignorance is just as bad.

—Bob Edwards,
National Public Radio Commentator

Curiosity is the wick in the candle of learning.

—William A. Ward,
Author

I don't divide the world into the weak and the strong, or the successes and the failures, those who make it and those who don't. I divide the world into learners and non-learners.

—Benjamin Barber,
Author, Political Theorist

———————

To be conscious that you are ignorant of the facts is a great step to knowledge.

—Benjamin Disraeli,
Former British Prime Minister

———————

Most people are mirrors, reflecting the moods and emotions of the times; few are windows, bringing light to bear on the dark corners where troubles fester. The whole purpose of education is to turn mirrors into windows.

—Sydney J. Harris,
Columnist

———————

Never regard study as a duty, but as the enviable opportunity to learn to know the liberating influence of beauty in the realm of the spirit for your own personal joy and to the profit of the community to which your later work belongs.

—Albert Einstein

If your plan is for 1 year, plant rice; if your plan is for 10 years, plant trees; if your plan is for 100 years, educate children.

—Confucius

Through education, we have the ability to change and improve the world in which we live. By touching the lives of students, outstanding educators make the future brighter for all of us.

—Alaska Governor
Tony Knowles

In this century, we have weathered two world wars, several other international conflicts, a major depression, several recessions, mounting global competition, and rapid social change. Yet somehow, the graduates of your schools—despite all the defects attributed to them—have managed to create the most powerful, successful nation on earth.

—Sam Salva,
Former Executive
Director, NAEP

The rewards of teaching come from teachers' innate belief that every day they have the opportunity to enrich the lives of their students by igniting the human spirit, dignifying the human experience, and inspiring human excellence.

—John Blaydes,
Educator, Author,
Motivational Speaker

Education stands firmly as the cornerstone of our great nation. A commitment to education is a commitment to our children and their future. Our children are our most precious resource and we, as citizens and communities, must never forget that the skills and knowledge we provide our children with today will become the foundation of tomorrow. We must make certain that the opportunity for a quality education is available for all children. The dedication and tireless efforts put forth by our educators to enhance the learning process is essential to the growth and prosperity of our communities and our nation.

—Tom Ridge,
Former Pennsylvania Governor